Yeah, But Where Are You Really From?

Yeah, But Where Are You Really From?

A Story of Overcoming the Odds

MARGUERITE PENROSE

SANDYCOVE

an imprint of

PENGUIN BOOKS

SANDYCOVE

UK | USA | Canada | Ireland | Australia
India | New Zealand | South Africa

Sandycove is part of the Penguin Random House group of companies
whose addresses can be found at global.penguinrandomhouse.com.

Penguin
Random House
UK

First published 2022
001

Copyright © Marguerite Penrose, 2022

The moral right of the author has been asserted

Set in 13.5/16pt Garamond MT Std
Typeset by Jouve (UK), Milton Keynes
Printed and bound in Great Britain by Clays Ltd, Elcograf S.p.A.

The authorized representative in the EEA is Penguin Random House Ireland,
Morrison Chambers, 32 Nassau Street, Dublin DO2 YH68

A CIP catalogue record for this book is available from the British Library

ISBN: 978–1–844–88593–0

www.greenpenguin.co.uk

Penguin Random House is committed to a
sustainable future for our business, our readers
and our planet. This book is made from Forest
Stewardship Council® certified paper.

I dedicate this book to my amazing, loving parents, Noeline and Michael; to my wonderful sister, Ciara, and my nephews, Jamie and Charlie; as well as my birth mother, Elizabeth; my birth father, whose name I do not know; and any biological siblings I might have, in Ireland, Africa or elsewhere, whom I am yet to meet.

Contents

Prologue: Discovery

Because I am Black and my family are white, when people meet us for the first time, they often have a lot of questions. I frequently feel the need to interject with a quick explanation of how we belong together, because I can see the questions in their eyes, and I want to get it out of the way so that any awkwardness can be dissipated and we can move on.

Even though I was born and raised in Ireland – even though my childhood could not have *been* more Irish, with red lemonade and Holy Communion parties, ham sandwiches and bacon and cabbage, Thin Lizzy and U2 on the stereo, and a life firmly rooted in Dublin, the city where I grew up – when most people see me, they do not see an Irish woman. They see a Black woman with brown skin and black hair – and, often, they make a whole load of assumptions about me, that are nearly always completely wrong, just because of how I look.

A lot of people who grew up in adoptive families or in foster care suffer from feelings of not ever having quite fitted in, and experience sensations of anxiety or of longing to know and be part of their biological families. Sometimes these feelings haunt them for their whole lives, as they wonder about how things might have been. I am not one of those people, and I never have been, because I have an absolutely fantastic adoptive family – with parents who have always encouraged me to achieve all I can, with a sister who is also my best friend – and I have always known that I am cherished, loved and special. For most of my daily life, the fact that I was fostered, and then adopted, was not something that I ever experienced as negative.

Still, at the back of my mind, I have often wondered about the people who gave me life, and as I went through my forties – and especially after a health emergency that nearly killed me – I started to want to know much more about the woman who gave birth to me, and the man who is my biological father. What did they look like? What sort of people were they? Were they glad that they had come together to give me life? Did they ever think of me and wish me the best? Did they wonder how my life had worked out, and hope I had been successful in my career? Or was I just a mistake that they had made, and had spent the rest of their lives trying to forget, while regretting the very fact of my existence? For the first time, when I looked in the mirror I saw not just my own familiar face, but also the puzzle of who I am and where I come from.

I signed up online with the National Adoption Preference Registry for biological parents and adoptees, in the hope of finding a match. The registry was set up in 2005, and it gives everyone who was adopted in Ireland, as well as everyone from the birth family of someone who was adopted, the opportunity to list their details and state what sort of contact they would like to have with one another, if any. Some people might just want information about their biological family's medical history, while others might be hoping for a full relationship with their birth mothers and fathers, and even all of their relatives. I got my confirmation letter back from the online registry quite quickly and have not heard anything since.

I also applied to Tusla, the Irish child and family agency

established in 2014, and about a year later, they contacted me to let me know that I could start the process of finding out about my biological family. Then I received a call from one of their employees. I panicked when I picked up the phone and realized what the call was about because, suddenly, I was not sure that I really did want to know, after all. I had a strong feeling that my biological mother was no longer alive, and I didn't know if I was ready to have that confirmed and to have to deal with whatever emotions got dragged to the surface. There were so many other things to think about too. What if my birth relatives had been contacted and did not want to meet me? What if they *did* want to meet me, and then we did not like each other? What if it all went horribly wrong, and meeting me set off a domino effect that brought nothing but harm to countless people? I had joined a number of online forums for adoptees and, reading their stories, I knew that many of them had had difficult, and even traumatic, experiences of meeting their birth relatives. I knew that it was rarely easy, and was often extremely painful. What I did not know was whether or not I was ready for it.

'D'you know what?' I said to the Tusla caseworker. 'I'll leave it for the moment.'

'That's fine,' she said kindly. 'It's entirely up to you. If you ever change your mind, you know where we are.'

After putting the phone down, I wondered again about how many adopted people had signed up with Tusla, how many of them had contacted their biological relatives, and how the contact usually went. Then life went on, and I put all the questions to the back of my mind, deciding that I would revisit them only when and if I felt ready to.

About five years later, shut into my apartment because of Covid and cut off from friends and family, knowing that I was a lot more vulnerable than the average person because I have a chronic disability and a complex medical history, I started thinking a lot more about myself and my biological family. That summer in 2020, I found an Instagram feed called Black and Irish, which featured a few stories of people with backgrounds a bit like mine. Reading these, I felt a huge sense of kinship to them, and enormously grateful to those who had created a forum enabling us to find our voices and share our stories. So I did something that I had not done since I was in school: I started to write.

I wrote all about myself and what it had been like growing up as a little Dublin girl with brown skin and wild black curls, and the many things that have happened to me over the years.

About being the only person of colour in my Irish family, with their Celtic looks, their freckles, their pale skin, and the strong likenesses that pass from one generation to the next, and that fascinate us all as we pore over old photographs and welcome each new baby into the clan.

About the way people had responded to me and my appearance over the years – with curiosity, with animosity, even sometimes with naked racism.

About living with a disability that modern surgery has been unable to repair and how, if it had not been for my parents, I would have grown up in an institution such as an orphanage or a children's home.

About how, perhaps, if I had not been adopted, eventually the loneliness and my complex medical needs might even have brought my story to an early end, because without my adoptive family, I am sure that I would never have received the care and attention I needed as a child, even if the nurses had done their absolute best.

4

I wrote and wrote and, when I had finished, I sent it all to the people who run the Black and Irish Instagram feed. I honestly thought that I might never hear from them again, and was just glad to have been given the push to think about myself and write it all down. But, to my amazement, they got back in touch with me very quickly.

'We think your piece is great!' they said. 'We'd like to edit it a little, but we'd love to feature it on our page.'

I could hardly believe it.

'God yeah,' I said. 'Of course.'

Nothing could have prepared me for what was going to happen next. The article was published online within a week, and within a few minutes of its being posted, I started to receive notifications from Instagram and from all the people who had read it and who wanted to get in touch, to comment on my story, and share theirs.

I had not given much thought to what it would feel like to send my story out into the world and, to be honest with you, it was completely overwhelming. I was in work as the notifications poured in, and I remember sitting at my desk and shaking, unable even to click a tab on my computer screen to see what was happening in the Instagram feed. I felt exposed and vulnerable, and was sort of amazed at what I had done because, while most of the people who know me consider me very confident and outgoing, I am actually quite a private person at heart.

Fortunately, most of the comments and questions were friendly and kind. People wrote in to say that my story was fascinating, that it had given them insight into what it was like being Black and Irish, and that they wished me all the best in my life. There were one or two negative comments (aren't there always?), but they were drowned out by the sea of positivity. I realized that my story really resonated with a lot of people. An interview on *The Ryan Tubridy Show* followed. There was a huge reaction to what I had to say. Incredibly, among those who got in touch was a woman called Catherine, who remembered me as an infant in the mother and baby home. Finally, at the age of forty-six, I started to learn the answers to my many questions about who I really am.

Mam, my adoptive mother, has always told me that I should talk more about myself. Because I am genuinely interested in others and love hearing their stories, and perhaps because for many years I was quite reluctant to share mine, there were things about my life that I rarely mentioned, even to my family or close friends. For most of my life, for example, I had not wanted to talk about what it is like being Black and Irish, or even to think about it very much, because I felt that the way I look is just who I am, and that it is one of the least important things about me. Nobody can choose the colour of their skin, so what does it matter? I thought. Who cares? Nor had I ever talked much about my scoliosis and the many ways in which it has impacted on my self-image, my health and my plans, because I have spent a lifetime enjoying an active, full existence and never letting my disability hold me back. I even find it difficult to use the word 'disabled' about myself, because I know that a lot of people are in a much more challenging situation than me.

But now, having started to share my story on the Black and Irish feed – which in turn led to a lot of publicity, to new opportunities to learn more about who I am and where I come from – I thought, Well, why not simply share it all? Why not put pen to paper and lay it all out there?

I am just one woman who has never been in the public eye

before, but the circumstances of my birth and adoption, the wonderful family life with which I have been blessed, and my experience as a child born into Irish institutional care, as a Black Irish woman, and as an active, happy person with a significant disability, all shed light in unexpected ways on our shared history as a nation, as Irish people, and – I sincerely believe – on how we can work together to make our society a better and more nurturing place for everyone.

So, here I am. This is me.

1. Difficult to Place

My name, which I have always loved, was given to me – I assume – by my biological mother when I was born, and it is the only thing that connects me with her and with my earliest childhood memories, when together with two other children with disabilities, I lived in the 'reject room' of an institution.

On 19th January 1974, I was born to a young woman called Elizabeth in one of Ireland's infamous mother and baby homes, St Patrick's on the Navan Road in North Dublin. The large, forbidding red-brick building was one of the main mother and baby homes in the city at the time. It had been operating as such since the early twentieth century and was run by a religious order called the Daughters of Charity of Saint Vincent de Paul, who oversaw the care of young, pregnant women and their babies at a time when unmarried women and their children were seen as damaged goods, as bringing shame on their families, and even as threatening the fabric of Irish society, to be kept out of sight and away from polite company.

In recent years, we have learned that many of the women in St Patrick's were brutally mistreated, and that for much of its history, the mortality rate among the infants was extremely high. For the surviving children born there, the only route to a happy ending was adoption, but largely because of anxiety about people adopting a baby of the 'wrong' faith, there was no legal adoption in Ireland until 1954, just twenty years before I was born. Instead, Catholic American families often adopted Irish babies – they liked to adopt Irish children because Ireland was poor then and they felt that they were giving them a good chance and, in some cases, because they wanted to be sure of getting a baby that was a hundred per cent white, because America is such a melting pot that adoptive parents there ran the 'risk' of taking on a baby that might later turn out to be of mixed parentage.

Most of these adoptive parents wanted nothing but the best for the children they took into their families, I imagine – but the bottom line is that the majority of these children were purchased, in all but name. And when a child becomes a commodity, with a monetary value, there is a big incentive for anyone with few scruples to make good money from the suffering of their birth mothers.

For most of the history of the home where I started my life, the few mixed-race babies who were born there were not even put up for adoption, but moved into the industrial school system as soon as they were old enough. Like the mother and baby homes, the industrial schools have, in recent years, been the subject of a great deal of scrutiny, because in many cases the children who grew up in them were physically and sexually abused, poorly fed and educated, and exploited for their labour. Together with children with disabilities and serious illnesses, mixed-race children were seen as inferior, and the assumption was that nobody would want to adopt them, and still less part with their hard-earned cash for an opportunity to take these children into their families. Generations of children with skin the 'wrong' colour, and children with disabilities, grew up without loving families, with nobody to take pride in their milestones, nobody to encourage them to achieve all they could, nobody to tell them that they were loved. Many of them were neglected and even abused. Many of them died.

By the mid-1970s, when I was born, conditions for children in the mother and baby homes were better than they had been before, although they were still very poor, and in terms of social work and human rights, Ireland was moving – slowly – in the right direction. But for my generation of mother-and-baby-home children, and for their mothers, it was nonetheless a very different world to today.

Elizabeth was born in 1945 into a large working-class family in the southside of Dublin, near the Grand Canal. She had five older brothers and one or possibly two younger sisters – my caseworker is unable to confirm. Elizabeth's mam and dad were getting quite elderly, and her father had experienced a lot of ill health, including a number of hospitalizations for cancer.

We hear about the women and girls who got pregnant and ended up in the homes, and about the babies they gave up – but for every baby that was born in those places, there was a father too and we hear much less about them. I know that some of those men had abandoned the women they had made pregnant, that some of those women were probably raped by the fathers of their children, and that some of the men never knew that they were fathers, but I also know that some of the fathers did their absolute best to gain custody of their children, and that they were cruelly rejected by the religious orders.

I do not know the name of my biological father. My adoptive parents and I have been told that he came from Zambia and that he spent time at the Irish Army barracks on the Curragh, together with a number of other African cadets. The story goes that he and my mother had a relationship for about eight months, after which he went home. I have no way of knowing if what I have been told about him is actually true. The information about the fathers of children in the mother and baby homes is often inaccurate. However, the paperwork that I have seen describes my father as Zambian. That detail is all I have to help me in my efforts to track him down.

I have been led to believe that my biological parents met at a dance hall, the two of them presumably dressed up for the night out, and excited to meet an attractive stranger. My father was probably the first Black man Elizabeth had ever encountered. Maybe he told her stories about his life back home, thrilling her with details that would have seemed exciting to a young woman who might never have travelled outside Ireland. I can imagine all I like, but I have to accept I will probably never know.

Elizabeth was twenty-nine years old when she became pregnant. I imagine that her family were not happy to learn that she was expecting a baby without a husband in sight, and that they were, at the very least, taken aback to learn that the father was a Black African man. There is no way for me to know how Elizabeth's family reacted, and whether they were supportive of her or angry about the pregnancy. There were very few Black people in Ireland at that time – mostly just students from former British colonies studying subjects like medicine and engineering at Trinity College – so the very idea of their daughter having a baby with a Black man must have seemed strange, and even shocking, to Elizabeth's parents. It is possible, too, that my father already had a wife at home, and was therefore not in a position to marry Elizabeth.

Things were beginning to change for the better in Ireland, but unmarried mothers were still considered fallen women, even then, and most Irish people had never met a Black person, let alone welcomed one into the family. What little they knew about Africa they had generally learned from the back of the Trócaire box, which was distributed to Irish families during Lent, so that they could save money to send to the missions overseas.

At some point during her pregnancy, Elizabeth may have stayed at the St Patrick's mother and baby home, perhaps because her family were upset about the situation, because she felt alone and unsupported, because she felt coerced into doing so, or because she genuinely wanted to be there. Once the decision for me to be born into the home had been taken, the assumption would have been that Elizabeth would give me up. Pregnant women walked through the doors of the home, and when they left, their babies stayed behind. That is just how it was.

I have been told that Elizabeth and my father were in contact during her pregnancy and that he returned later at some point, when he visited me in St Patrick's. Apparently, he suggested that custody be granted to him so that he could take me back to his family and raise me in Zambia. This would have been out of the question for the nuns who ran the home and had complete authority over it and all the women and babies within: for one thing, it was seen as a priority to ensure that all of the children had a Catholic upbringing, and for another, in those days people thought of Africa as a place of constant, unremitting poverty and starvation, and nothing else – and of Black people as less 'civilized' than white people – and they would have felt that keeping me in Ireland was safer and would give me a better chance in life.

I have always wondered if my father, who is said to have sought custody of me, thought about me much over the years. Did he ask himself what my life was like? Hope that I was being raised by kind people who would see my potential and nourish it? Worry that I would be treated badly because of the dark skin that I have inherited from him? Miss me and wish that we could be together? There is no way for me to tell.

For so much of the history of the homes, the religious orders stood to make very good money arranging for the babies to be adopted by couples who were often wealthy, and who were also sure that they had the God-given right to claim other people's children. I find it difficult to comprehend how the Irish state, and so many Irish people, seem to have been complicit in handing complete control over the lives of mothers and children to organizations, with no oversight at all.

In earlier years, unmarried mothers gave birth in the mother and baby homes, and many of them were treated extremely harshly, and even taunted as they gave birth, told that God was punishing them and that their pains in childbirth were the price they paid for their sins. By the 1970s, however, when they went into labour they were brought to give birth in maternity hospitals. I was born in St James's Hospital in Dublin's inner city, and I hope and trust that Elizabeth was treated kindly while she was in labour, and given all the help she needed, even though there was no nervous, excited husband in the waiting room, ready to kiss her and cry happy tears over their little baby.

As soon as I was born, it was clear that being mixed-race in an overwhelmingly white society was not going to be the only challenge I would face, or even the biggest. I had severe congenital scoliosis, which meant that my spine was crooked and that my torso had not formed properly, and I was missing several ribs, so my organs were all rather crowded inside my tiny frame. Clearly, I was going to need surgery and there would be lifelong consequences for my health.

All of these differences that made me who I am would also have major consequences for how others saw me: not just as Marguerite, but as a person with a number of labels attached to her. These labels would impact on others' perception and treatment of me for the rest of my life: Black, mixed-race, disabled. To these the circumstances of my birth added another label: ward of state.

Immediately after my birth, as planned, Elizabeth relinquished custody of me and handed me over to the state. I don't know how long she stayed in hospital after I was born: possibly she had to go home with milk still in her swollen breasts, still wearing pads for the post-birth bleeding, and had to deal with the discomfort on her own. I have no idea what she felt about all this. Was she sad? Relieved? Regretful? Worried? No woman really wants to give up her child, but in Elizabeth's situation she would have felt that she was doing the right thing. In Ireland in those days, support for unmarried mothers was minimal, and people were often very judgemental. It would have been extremely difficult for Elizabeth to raise me on her own.

The records do show that Elizabeth continued to visit me after giving me up, although they don't indicate how often. I hope that the nuns in the home were kind to her when she visited and that they gave her the time and space she needed to get to know, and say goodbye to, her little daughter, but I have no reason to assume that they were. It is hard to believe that she would have been encouraged to come very often, as the authorities would not have wanted a bond to form between mother and child, making the whole situation even more difficult than it already was. The mother and baby homes do not have a history of being compassionate towards the mothers who passed through their doors, or even of keeping proper records about them. What I think I know about my first weeks is based on the assumption that my records are accurate.

I have no way of knowing whether or not the medical records from birth that I obtained only recently are complete. One thing that grates is the fact that whoever filled them in generally got my name wrong and referred to me as 'Margaret' not 'Marguerite'. It is hurtful because it makes me feel that they were not really thinking about the little girl in front of them but rather just going through the motions – and it hurts because my name is so special to me.

I do believe that Elizabeth loved me and was confident that she was doing the best she could by leaving me somewhere I would be cared for, in the hope that I would be adopted by a loving family in due course. I have never felt rejected by her, just sad that we did not have the opportunity to meet, and hopeful that she went on to have a happy and fulfilling life without me, her first child.

I have just a few memories from my very early days at St Patrick's. I remember being in my cot, looking through the bars at a little boy of my own age called Philip. I have a hazy recollection of Philip just always being there, beside me, close enough for us to reach out and touch one another's hands. There were three of us in the room: me, Philip and a little girl called Clara. Because we all had medical issues, we were kept apart from the other children and not even offered to prospective adoptive parents, as the feeling was that nobody would want to take on a child with such serious problems. I do not know what health issues Philip and Clara had, but presumably we all had what were seen as limitations of some sort.

In my case, not only did I have severe scoliosis and

associated health issues, but I was Black too: I think the assumption was that nobody would want me, and that I would have to grow up in an institution. In a way I was fortunate, because just a generation earlier, disabled and otherwise unwell children in institutional care in Ireland were often effectively left to die, and then – as now we all know – sometimes buried with little to no ceremony in unmarked graves and even, in the case of the infamous Bon Secours mother and baby home in Tuam, in a disused septic tank.

I believe that I was treated relatively well at the home, in terms of receiving good practical and medical care. I was fed, dressed and kept healthy and clean, and I know that many of the carers were kind women who were doing their best. I have no reason to think that I was abused or actively mistreated in any way. But no child deserves to be raised in an institution, and many children who spend their first years in care are left with psychological scars that make the rest of their lives difficult. They can find it hard to bond with others, and often feel very insecure in their relationships with the people they love the most. They have higher than average levels of anxiety, depression and relationship breakdown.

I have always been a very positive person, I have always felt extremely secure in my close relationships, and I love getting to know people and find it easy to trust them. I had often wondered why I was so resilient – why had those earliest years of my life apparently left me with little psychological trauma?

After *The Ryan Tubridy Show*, and contacting Catherine, the woman who had cared for me in St Patrick's, she and I stayed in touch. Following a few long phone calls, we agreed to meet, and I arranged to go to her home in Wexford together with my mam and dad and sister Ciara, who were also anxious to meet her – they knew no more about my very early life than I did and wanted to support me on a journey that might prove to be emotionally demanding.

I had no conscious memory of Catherine, but when she opened the door of her house, I warmed to her immediately. She welcomed us all in, made us tea, and told us to help ourselves from the huge spread of food and cakes that she had laid out. Just as my mother always does for visitors, Catherine had prepared enough food to feed an army. My parents and sister found it just as easy as I had to talk to Catherine, and it felt wonderful, but slightly surreal, to be sitting together around her table, knowing that I was the catalyst that had brought us together, and inspired her to tell us her story. When I look back now I can see that I was so stunned by it all that I simply sat and listened most of the time.

Catherine was just eighteen when she started working at St Patrick's, and she was put in charge of me, Philip and Clara. Soon she and I had formed a close bond. St Patrick's had attractive grounds, and Catherine asked if she could take me out into the garden to play on the grass, as I had never been out of doors before, and she was given permission to do so. As she became more confident with me, she asked the nuns if she could take me home to her family once in a while, and they said yes.

'We all loved you at home,' Catherine said. 'You were such a little dote. You were so tiny; you were like a living doll. And although you were withdrawn, you smiled at me.'

The family home was full and they had no cot for me, so Catherine's dad pulled one of the drawers out of a chest of drawers, and made a cosy bed for me there that I fitted into very tidily. Soon I was spending weekends with Catherine and her family.

Catherine did not earn a lot of money, but she used some of it to buy me outfits, tops and clips for my hair, and she liked dressing me up and making me look pretty. One day, when I was about eighteen months old, or maybe two, she took me on a bus for the first time. She carried me upstairs to the top deck and laughed in delight as I squealed with excitement about what we saw. Catherine became so fond of me, she even imagined adopting me herself, but as a young, single woman just starting out in her career, it was out of the question.

After she had been working at St Patrick's for a year and a half, some of Catherine's friends, who were studying nursing in England, persuaded her to join them there, and she squeezed me goodbye for the last time and left my life until over forty years later, when she happened to be listening to *The Ryan Tubridy Show* just when I was talking to him about my experiences. Catherine had returned to Ireland after a few years in England, and said that whenever she had seen a dark-skinned girl in Dublin it had reminded her of me. She had never forgotten me or stopped wishing me well.

Eventually, our afternoon in Catherine's cosy kitchen and beautiful garden came to an end, and my family and I said our goodbyes. Catherine insisted on giving Dad a rose plant from her garden, and as we all got into the car, we promised that we would stay in touch. Like an old friend, Catherine stood and waved us off as we drove away. When we got home, Dad planted Catherine's rose in his garden; it is thriving in the sunny spot that he chose.

I wish I could remember some of those happy times I spent with Catherine, but I do not. However, I do know that they made all the difference in the world to me. In the first years of a child's life, their brain is growing and developing at an incredible rate. A child who knows that someone loves them unconditionally, who has someone to trust, someone who holds them and cuddles them, will learn at that early stage that life is not all about hard knocks and that there are good people out there who care.

By loving me then, Catherine made it so much easier for me to love others as my childhood progressed. I am so grateful to her for all she did for me at that time.

What Catherine did not learn until decades later – till that day she heard me on the radio – is that soon after she left St Patrick's to seek opportunities in England, my life changed for ever.

2. Michael and Noeline

Michael and Noeline Penrose were a young Dublin couple in their early twenties. Michael had grown up in Baldoyle, and Noeline was from Raheny, which are both suburbs on the northside of the city. They met at a dance when Noeline was sixteen and Michael just a year older, both dressed to the nines in the latest sixties fashions, and they had been together ever since. Both were from warm, loving families from similar hard-working backgrounds: Noeline's father had a good job at Cadbury's, and Michael's worked in ship-building. Noeline had one sister and two brothers, and Michael had three brothers. Michael started out working in MacPherson's paint factory, and Noeline had begun her working life in a factory before getting an office job. They got married in 1971, at twenty and twenty-one, Michael proud in his suit and Noeline in a full-length white wedding dress with her hair done by her sister Angela, who was a hair-dresser, and renowned in the family for being glamorous and for her sense of style.

By the time I was born to Elizabeth in 1974, Noeline and Michael were living in their own house in Howth, another northside suburb, and were expecting their first baby. Photographs show Michael with a big seventies moustache and an exuberant head of dark hair, while Noeline was tall and slender with long, mid-brown hair. They were a very attractive couple. Three months after I came into the world, Noeline gave birth to a beautiful little girl whom they called Ciara.

Noeline had a dreadful time with the pregnancy and birth and, although she loved Ciara to pieces, she knew that she did not want to go through all that again. Fortunately for Noeline, and thanks in large part to the women's liberation movement, which was then doing great work in Ireland, it was getting easier for women to plan their families, rather than simply putting up with one pregnancy after another, regardless of how much they suffered.

One day in 1977, Michael went to lunch at his Auntie Molly's house, just across the railway track from MacPherson's. While he was there, he met one of her neighbours, Mona, who worked at St Patrick's mother and baby home as a nurse. Mona, a warm and approachable young woman who was a good friend of Molly's and of Molly's daughters, told Michael all about the little children there who had not been adopted or fostered yet. Mona was a kind woman with a big heart, and she was doing her best to make things better for the children born into the home, and for their mothers.

'They'd break your heart,' Mona said now. 'The little mites.'

There was a new system in place, Mona said, for the kids in long-term care at St Patrick's to go into temporary foster arrangements, just for the Christmas holidays, so that they could have a taste of what a real family Christmas was like.

'I don't suppose you'd be interested, would you?' she asked Michael. 'Yourself and Noeline? You've plenty of room.'

Mona took a photograph out of her pocket and showed it to Michael. The blurry image showed a little girl sitting on a rocking horse.

'Maybe you could take her out for Christmas?' Mona asked. 'She's a lovely wee thing and I've got very fond of her.'

Because Mona's working hours were long and she lived some distance from the home, she often stayed the night there in the nurses' accommodation, and she had spent a lot of time playing with the children. She explained now that she sometimes took the little girl in the photo home, that she had already played all over Mona and Molly's houses, and that she was a friendly child once you got to know her.

'Don't see why not,' Michael said.

Mona gave Michael the photograph, and he went back home and told Noeline about the conversation.

'This is her picture,' he said. 'This is the little girl.'

Noeline was standing at the sink peeling potatoes and she just glanced at the image. The quality of the photo was quite poor, but she could see that the little girl was 'coloured', as people said in those days.

'She has no one,' Michael said persuasively. 'And there's something wrong with her back.'

Neither Noeline nor Michael had to think about it much, as they had always felt that they would like to be foster parents and had often discussed the possibility. The idea had become more real when friends of theirs had started to foster a little boy whom they took out for the weekends and holidays. Moreover, as Noeline definitely did not want to go through pregnancy and birth again, they had already started talking about maybe adopting another child, although they had no concrete plans as yet. Fostering a little one from St Patrick's would give them the opportunity to see if they felt ready for opening up their family.

Shortly after that, Michael and Noeline went up to St Patrick's to meet the nun in charge of the home, Sister Rosemary, who took their details and told them to come back on Christmas Eve to collect their new foster child. Sister Rosemary was a pleasant, kind and smiling woman but, having been through the convent-school system as a girl, Noeline felt a little intimidated by the environment – the high ceilings, the simply furnished rooms, and the sterile smell, like a hospital. She noticed how clean and shiny the place was – 'You could've eaten your dinner off the floors,' she would say later. 'You could see your shadow in the shine.' She also noticed the deep silence. Although it was a mother and baby home, there was no chatter of women at work, and no sound of babies and toddlers crying or playing. It was as though there was nobody there at all. Now we know that the girls who went to the homes to have their babies often spent hours on end on their hands and knees, scrubbing those floors within an inch of their lives, and that little attention was given to their emotional needs.

But then Mona turned into the long corridor, holding the hand of a tiny girl with brown skin and black curls in a puff around her head and – just like that – Noeline and Michael fell in love with her. That little girl was me, and meeting the Penroses was the best thing that could ever have happened to me.

'Say hello to your mammy and daddy!' Sister Rosemary said that day.

I was a very shy, withdrawn little thing, and just looked up at Noeline and Michael through my eyelashes.

'You were just a dote,' Mam always says when she remembers the first time she set eyes on me. 'You were so small you were hardly there, but you were so cute, and I knew straight away that I wanted you and that we had a space for you in our family.'

There was a hiccup on Christmas Eve when I had a chest infection and had to stay in the home, but two days later, on Stephen's Day, Mam and Dad were given a bag with my few bits and pieces in it and then they brought me home to their house in Donaghmede, where they had moved with Ciara. Mam says that I was very obedient and quiet, too quiet, and that I spent a lot of time sucking two of my fingers – I sucked my fingers so much and so hard that there was a huge dent in them – and just watching everything going on around me with my huge dark eyes. Because I was not used to interacting with people, I stood in the corner and looked at them. Mam put me in a bed in Ciara's room so that I would not be lonely.

'You were the talk of the town,' Mam says when she remembers that first Christmas. 'Everyone wanted to meet you.' All the neighbours were keen to come and say hello.

By the time Christmas was over, Noeline and Michael had decided that they wanted me to be part of their family not just for Christmas, but for ever.

'We had to get you out of there,' Mam said when she told me about making the decision to take me permanently. 'You were getting bigger, and we knew that if we didn't take you then, they'd be moving you on to an industrial school, and you were so small, you'd never have been able to stand up for yourself or deal with the rough and tumble. We needed to begin the process of fostering you.'

Mam had been taken by Mona to see the huge nursery where most of the small babies were kept. There were dozens of them, in rows in their cots. These were the children who were offered to prospective adoptive parents, but not all of them were chosen and if I was moved on to a bigger institution I would have to grapple for space with a lot of able-bodied kids who were bigger and stronger than me. Mam worried that I just would not be able to cope.

Whereas 'illegitimate' children had been casually boarded out and placed in institutions for generations with little or no interest in their well-being, by the late 1970s the system had improved. Now that they were looking for a long-term placement, Mam and Dad had to deal with mountains of paperwork and lots of interviews with social workers and other professionals. There were multiple home visits to make sure that I was going to a suitable environment, endless application forms to fill in, and formal interviews to be attended.

'They were only short of asking us what we had for breakfast,' Mam says when she remembers this process.

I find some comfort in knowing that the system was more stringent by the time I was three, and that the authorities were doing their best to ensure that foster children were going to families that would love them and care for them. I know that I was very fortunate not to have been born some years earlier when the checks were much less rigorous.

Although Mam and Dad had to tell the authorities absolutely everything about themselves, they were told very little in return about my biological parents; just that my father was Zambian and possibly in the medical corps of the Zambian Army, and that my mother was Irish and from south Dublin, near the Grand Canal. Mona filled in a few more details, saying that my father had been a tall Black man who wore a trench coat, as was fashionable at the time, and that he had come to see me at least twice at the home when I was little, even though, as a general rule, the fathers of the babies were not listed on the birth certificates and were not allowed to step through the doors. A letter from the authorities described my mother as an attractive, intelligent young woman with dark hair and a sallow complexion.

While all of this was going on, Mam and Dad were gradually getting to know me better. At first they were allowed to take me for the weekends. I would cry when they took me home on a Friday, and cry again when they brought me back on the Sunday. In the beginning, I seemed to be unsure of how to do anything. Dinner would be put in front of me, but I did not really know how to hold a fork or spoon and eat it. I had some repetitive behaviours, like rocking myself for comfort, which I had clearly learned from playmates with intellectual disabilities in the home; I stopped doing this soon after joining the Penroses.

I had already had a number of surgeries during early childhood, and soon in the fostering process I spent several weeks in hospital recovering from an operation to remove an obstruction at the base of my spine. While I was there, Mam and Dad learned that one of my doctors and his wife, who was a nurse at the same hospital, had also expressed an interest in fostering me. I had grown fond of the doctor, who was obviously very kind to me, and even pushed Dad away one day when he came to visit me, in favour of the doctor. Mam was worried that, because of my complex medical needs, the authorities would feel I would be better off with a couple with medical training who would understand and be able to participate in my treatment.

'They'll never let us have her,' Mam fretted. 'They're bound to choose medical people over us.'

But the social worker in charge of my case reassured Mam that she would never let that happen, especially as she had seen how close a bond I had formed with the whole Penrose family.

Although I had been brought back to St Patrick's after Christmas, once it had been decided that I was going to stay with the Penroses long-term, I started visiting for lengthier periods, even while I was still undergoing medical procedures.

At about three and a half, I spent time in St Vincent's Hospital having three artificial ribs made of titanium put in to replace the plastic ones that had been inserted in an earlier surgery. Because there was not enough space in my body for my lungs to expand properly, I had started having a lot of chest infections, and opening up my chest cavity more had become an emergency, before I began getting sick even more often and developing a serious health issue. My new metal ribs were an experimental treatment, and were actually made by a dentist, as he seems to have been the only person in Ireland at the time with the expertise for that sort of medical implant. He must have done a good job, because I still have the same three artificial ribs, over forty years later, and I expect to have them for the rest of my life.

Eventually, as my condition stabilized, Mam and Dad were told that I had been cleared to stay with them indefinitely. Mam tells me that, as one of the nuns at the home handed me over to her for the last time, she suggested Mam and Dad might like to change my name now that I was going to be staying with them long-term. She said that, as I was still very small, I would soon forget my old name and learn how to answer to a new one. They might like to give me a name that sounded more Irish, she said, especially considering the fact that I did not look like other Irish children with my brown skin and tight curls. Why make things more difficult than they had to be?

'You could just call her "Margaret",' the nun said. 'That's similar enough that she'll hardly notice the difference, and it would help her to fit in more. She could be "Maggie" for short.'

Mam was horrified at the thought of changing my name. I was only three, but I was already my own little person, and

I knew who I was. I knew that I was Marguerite. She also thought of the woman who had given birth to me, and presumably given me the name that she felt was right. It would be wrong, Mam said, to take away from me the only thing that I had from my mother. So Marguerite I remained.

When I look at photographs of myself from that time, I seem to remember snippets of it, but I am not sure if my memories are real, or if they are just reconstructed from the images and from what I have been told. Sometimes, when I walk into a doctor's or a dentist's waiting room, the scent of disinfectant gives me an emotional push, as though my mind is trying to summon memories from my early childhood in St Patrick's that I cannot quite access because they are buried beneath all the other things that have happened since.

I would absolutely love to remember those days clearly, but it does not really matter that I do not, because Mam and Dad – as I had already learned to call them – remember them for me, as do the many relatives on both sides of the family who opened their hearts to me from the very start.

3. A Loving Family

My life with the Penroses was the happy ending to my challenging start at the mother and baby home, and the happy beginning of what was a wonderful childhood that has given me more than enough joyful memories for a lifetime.

We were almost exactly the same age, so Ciara was also nearly four when I arrived on the scene. She and I bonded straight away, and we remained very close throughout our childhood. More than anything, this is an amazing testimony to what great parents we had. Looking back now, I can see how easy it would have been for everything to go horribly wrong.

Young as she was, who could have blamed Ciara for seeing this new arrival as a cuckoo in the nest? She had had her own bedroom, and now she had to share it with me. She had had all of her parents' attention just for herself, and now she had to share that too. Everything that Ciara had had for her alone, was now also mine.

Young as I was, anyone would have understood if I had felt jealous or resentful of this other little girl, the 'real' daughter, who was the same age as me, but straighter and taller and with a striking resemblance to our mam. I was only little, but I am sure that on some level I already understood that, to the casual onlooker, I would never be seen as part of the family in quite the same way that Ciara was.

Mam and Dad had carefully prepared Ciara for the fact that I would be coming to live with them for ever, telling her that she was going to have a new sister and that we would be great friends. They explained to me that I was going to be their little girl now, and that I would never be going back to St Patrick's.

By the time I came to stay with the Penroses full-time, Ciara was excited and thrilled to no longer be an only child, and I was equally excited and thrilled to have been chosen by them to be their little girl. The fact that I had come into their family as a foster child was never hidden or treated like something embarrassing or shameful. It was just the story of how I became one of the Penroses. From the moment I arrived I was a beloved member of the clan. We have all been supporting one another ever since.

Our first childhood home together was a semi-detached three-bedroom house in a cul-de-sac in the suburb of Donaghmede, where Mam and Dad had moved after starting their married life in Howth. Donaghmede had once been a satellite village of Dublin, but by the 1970s it was increasingly built-up and popular both with young families and more settled older people, who had grown up in the area when it was still surrounded by green fields. Ours was a typical suburban Dublin house: the front door opened into a hall with stairs running up against the wall on the left; there was a living room to the front, dining room in the middle, and kitchen at the back; and upstairs there were two large bedrooms, a bathroom and a box room. Mam and Dad had built a conservatory at the rear for extra space and to enjoy the light. Outside, we had a big back garden and a helpful hole in the fence that made it easy for Ciara and me to get to the neighbours. A little boy called Shane lived in the house behind ours, and the three of us were always climbing through that hole in the fence.

Our cul-de-sac was a lovely place to start growing up in, with so little traffic that even small children could play in the street and in one another's gardens with just light supervision from their parents. I feel privileged to have started out there. The cul-de-sac was filled with children of about our age. As well as Shane from the road behind, I remember playing on the street for hours with our neighbours Victoria, Caroline and Martina. We went through phases of repeating the same games obsessively. One favourite that lasted for a while was 'making perfume'. We would all get jam jars from our mothers, stuff them with flowers from gardens and the street, and then fill them up to the brim with water.

The cul-de-sac was great for the adults too. Most of the people living there were young parents. For stay-at-home mothers, it was good to have other women to chat to and share the childcare with, and on warm evenings all of the parents poured out on to the street with deckchairs, cups of tea or cans of beer. They would sit and gossip, and talk about news and sports, while the children played around them until, eventually, someone's mammy realized that it was much later than they thought, and time for all the children to start getting ready for bed. There were also lots of impromptu street parties for events like St Patrick's Day, when it was often easier for us all to stay on our friendly street and celebrate by ourselves.

Mam was a full-time mother in those days, and she gave us girls all her attention. She was very creative: she made curtains for the house with her sewing machine, and she was very good at baking and cooking and wanted to pass those skills on to her daughters. Even when we were tiny, she sat us up at the counter in the kitchen and showed us how to bake. We learned how to sift flour for scones, how to carefully measure out and mix the sugar and baking soda and other ingredients for a cake, and how to tip in exactly the right amount of vanilla. I have never forgotten those early lessons, and I can still turn out a good cake, though maybe not quite as good as hers. Mam felt strongly that every child needed to learn basic housekeeping skills, so from an early age Ciara and I were taught how to use the washing machine, how to make our beds, and how to prepare meals.

I loved helping Mam and even enjoyed cleaning with her; it might seem odd, but there was nothing I liked better as a little girl than giving the whole bathroom a good scrub, perhaps because I had seen so much work of this sort being done when I was in the mother and baby home. Ciara's job was doing the hoovering, and she was not particularly fond of it, but I often had to be dragged away from the bathroom because I was spending so long making every inch of it gleam.

Ciara and I started school at Scoil Áine in Raheny when we were about five, following in Mam's footsteps, as she had gone there when she was little too. Mam had a Mini and she drove Ciara and me, and our friend Caroline from across the road, every day. I can still remember going into the classroom for the first time and seeing the rows of little tables and chairs, all the right size for small children. When we were a bit older, Ciara, Caroline and I got the school bus together.

We all wore the school uniform – little tartan skirts with a pinafore top that went under our regulation shirt and jumper. I was the only Black child in the school, and would always be aware that I looked different, but I loved the fact that we were all dressed the same, and especially that Ciara and I went to school in matching outfits. Although I was a few months older than Ciara, she was always much taller than me. I looked up to her and thought of her as my big sister – Ciara was a bit of a bossy-boots and I was happy to do what she wanted me to – and I always loved it when I grew into her clothes, or when we were dressed the same. Wearing the school uniform made me feel even closer to her than I usually did, because our clothes were identical, just in different sizes.

We had some lovely teachers. Obviously, the teachers knew that I had scoliosis, and that I might not be able to take part in physical activities to the same extent as the other girls, but they were always very good about making sure that I did not feel left out and that I gave everything a try. I particularly remember Miss Dickson, who taught Irish dancing. I absolutely loved dancing and danced whenever I could, but of course my scoliosis prevented me from doing it as much or as well as I would have liked, because my compressed lungs meant that I got out of breath very quickly, and I was also not always very steady on my feet. Miss Dickson let me do dance class at my own pace, stopping to catch my breath as often as I needed to.

Ciara and I were in the same class, but when we were little I was much quieter, and Ciara would try to do things for me, telling people what I was thinking and what I wanted. Eventually the school told Mam that they were going to have to separate us because, unless I learned to speak up for myself, I might never speak much at all. From then on, we were placed in different classes and the school's approach worked because I soon found my voice, and became quite a chatterbox, and I have not stopped using my voice since.

I loved school. I wanted to be friends with everyone I met, and soon I had friends from all the classes. I did not have a shy bone in my body, and it never occurred to me that someone might not want to talk to me – as a result, almost everyone welcomed my friendly advances. For me, school was a wonderful place full of smiles.

By this stage, Dad had gone to work with Uncle David, Mam's brother-in-law, who was married to Auntie Angela. Uncle David was an electrician, and he had opened an electrical goods shop, Grant Electrical, on the ground floor of Donaghmede Shopping Centre, which had been built to serve the broader community since all the new estates sprang up in the 1960s and 1970s. The shopping centre was a big square of a building that was nothing much to look at, but it was the heart of the community and one of the focal points around which our family life revolved. Because of his training, Uncle David worked in the back repairing TV sets, video players and other appliances, and Dad worked front-of-house doing sales and customer relations. They both got to know almost all the other shopkeepers in the centre, and Ciara and I loved going to visit Dad at work, not just to see him and Uncle David, but also because we could parade around visiting the other shops and getting lots of praise and little treats. We especially liked visiting a shop called Pride and Joy that seemed to sell everything. It was like Aladdin's cave to us, stuffed with fancy stationery, toys, and knitting and craft supplies. When we had some pocket money, or when Gaga, our maternal grandfather, slipped us a bit of cash, we raced up to Pride and Joy to spend it. Once, the shop-owner's mother had been left in charge and she chased Ciara and me out because some other children had been in earlier and stolen something. Gaga took our hands and marched us up to the shop to chastise the lady behind the counter and make sure that we were able to buy the 'fancy paper' that we adored. I also loved visiting the bookshop upstairs, and because the shopkeeper knew me well, she let me sit on the floor and leaf through the new books, with their fascinating stories and their tantalizing smell, for as long as I wanted. I have always loved the way a book can transport me to another world.

Dad loved football. He and his brother Brendan – Uncle Brendan – had been involved in setting up the Donaghmede Celtic football team, and were deeply connected with the club and the Football Association of Ireland, the FAI. When it was not too cold, Dad brought me to football training on a Thursday night. I would stand on the sidelines, all wrapped up, and cheer them on and, when they were finished playing, I was handed around, given treats and told how great I was. Soon I felt as though I was one of the lads, alongside the men. I loved those outings and the gruff kindness of Dad's friends. To this day, I have a huge love of football and can hold my own in any conversation about it (although Dad supports Liverpool and I support Manchester United, which can lead to some interesting discussions over Sunday dinner). Dad also had a huge passion for music although – God love him – he did not have a note in his head or an ounce of rhythm. On Sunday mornings, he would get out of bed and put the stereo on at full blast. He liked it all: rock, pop, classical, trad. He was a huge U2 fan, and so am I; I listened to enough of them when I was little! (When Dad got tickets to see the first *Joshua Tree* concert, I went with him. We drove there in a limo and I felt like a VIP. It was my first live concert, and I could not have been more excited.)

The final member of the family was our dog Mandy, a gentle red setter who put up with lots of vigorous love from Ciara and me. I think that Mandy was already there before I arrived, because I have no memory of a time before her.

Mandy was a very pampered pet and was given the run of the house. She was gentle and kind, and Ciara and I loved dragging her into our bedroom to involve her in our games. Poor Mandy probably had to attend hundreds of dolls' tea parties. We often played 'nurses and doctors', when my ample knowledge of doctors' appointments and hospitals came in handy. Mandy made an excellent patient.

Of course, much as I loved Ciara, my parents and the whole family, I knew that I was not quite the same as them. Mam and Dad dealt with the fact that Ciara and I were different in the best way possible, by acknowledging the differences between us and talking about them openly rather than by pretending they were not there. From an early age, they told me to ask any questions I wanted, and that they would always do whatever they could to help me find the answers. As a small child, I knew that I was free to discuss the fact that I was fostered whenever I needed to. I rarely had any questions, but when I did, Mam and Dad were always happy to answer them. Although they knew nothing about my biological parents, and although they had grown up at a time when – as Dad says – a woman or girl who got pregnant outside marriage was discussed as though she had committed a criminal act, they both spoke extremely highly of them. They said they were sure that my mother and father had done the best they could for me, and that they had wanted me to be raised by a loving family, because they were not able to bring me up themselves, for reasons that were beyond their control. They assured me that my parents would be very proud of me, if they could see what a great girl I was and how well I was doing, and that they were both certainly lovely people from whom I had inherited some of my best qualities. I was content with these explanations, as I loved my family so much, and would not wonder until I was older what it might have been like to grow up with other people. I rarely asked for information about my origins, and sometimes even put my hand up and walked away when someone referred to the fact that I had not always been with the Penroses, because I preferred not to know too much.

My parents had no idea then that many of the girls and women who went to St Patrick's had very little choice when it came to giving away their babies. They believed in good faith that my mother had voluntarily surrendered me for adoption, because she thought that this was the best thing to do. Of course, she may have done, and I certainly hope that she was happy with the decision and felt supported, but there is probably no way of knowing now. I hope that she was not one of the many who bitterly regretted the loss of her child, or who was bullied and strong-armed into handing me over by people who felt that they knew what was best for her.

Ciara and I were fortunate enough to still have all four grandparents alive, and I was very close to all of them. Mam's mother, Nana Josie, always took care of the two of us at her home in Raheny on Tuesdays. She had been a housewife all her life, and she was very proud of the home she kept and took good care of herself and her appearance. She was a slender lady, always impeccably dressed in a tidy outfit of a nice skirt, a blouse – with a cardigan if it was cold – and some discreet jewellery, like a string of pearls and a small pair of pearl earrings. Her hair was always perfectly set. Nana Josie told me that she had always wanted to have curly hair, and was envious of mine. She said that she loved my thick Afro hair, and was always touching it and caressing it. While Nana Josie made me feel very special, and I loved her dearly, I was ambivalent about all the attention she paid to my hair, as it reminded me that I was different. I could not see why she liked it so much, and would have preferred to have sleek, straight hair like my sister's.

Nana Josie got up early every morning and set to work, making sure that the house was absolutely spotless. Every bit of the place was vacuumed and dusted to within an inch of its life. All the furniture shone, and there was never even a speck of dust on any of the china tea sets and figurines that she kept in display cabinets in the living room. She had a specific dish that she liked to make for each day of the week. On Tuesdays, it was always a delicious stew. The juicy lumps of meat and sweet chunks of carrot tasted amazing in Nana Josie's house. If we were there on a Friday, there was homemade fish and chips.

Gaga, Mam's dad, had already retired and he was often at home too. Like Nana Josie, he took great pride in his appearance. He was usually dressed in a tidy pair of trousers and a formal blazer over a shirt, with a V-necked jumper and tie. Gaga was a great storyteller and I loved sitting on his knee to hear one of his tales or, sometimes, to watch television with him. I remember him being outraged when he learned that I had to study Irish at school, just like all the other children. I think he felt that, because of my colour, I should be exempt! Uncle Pat, Mam's unmarried brother, was still living at home, and was always very kind as well. He entertained us, and was a real character.

On sunny days, Ciara and I were let loose to play in Nana Josie's large back garden. In my memory, the summer was always hot and sunny when I was little, and when I think of that garden, I remember endless hours lying on the bright blankets that we brought outside to put on the grass, where we played with our toys, read, and chatted endlessly.

We also had a wonderful relationship with our Penrose grandparents, who lived in Old Baldoyle, about a half-hour's drive from us. When he was little, Dad had been raised largely by his grandmother, but this had not prevented him from developing a very close relationship with his parents, who were fantastic grandparents to Ciara and me. Nana Kitty, like Nana Josie, was always beautifully turned out and, even if she was just going to the local shop, she would do her hair, put on a bit of lipstick, and tie a stylish scarf around her head. In his younger days, Grandad Paddy had worked in shipbuilding in the UK, and he had plenty of stories to tell about when he worked away, and always spoiled us rotten. He was especially protective of me because I was small and delicate and different to the other kids.

I loved going to Nana Kitty's, because in her house there were no rules at all, and the children got to decide what they wanted to do. She felt that, as a granny, it was her job to indulge us, so she let Ciara and me stay up as late as we wanted, regardless of what our mammy said. When we stayed over, she gave us hot-water bottles and heaped up the blankets on our beds. She fed us wholesome Dublin fare – bacon, cabbage and, when they were in season, the delicious new potatoes that she described as 'balls of flour', laden with pools of melted butter. My dinner plate, when it was handed to me, would be piled so high that I could not see over it and had to eat a few forkfuls from the top before the people on the other side of the table came into view. Nearly every time we visited Nana Kitty, we left with a gift, because she was always so generous.

Ciara and I were not just part of a loving nuclear family, and not just blessed with four doting grandparents, but we were also members of a big extended family, with plenty of relatives on both sides, all of whom played an active role in our childhood. We had lots of cousins who were close in age. Our Auntie Angela, Mam's sister and Uncle David's wife, lived in Artane and we saw her and her family very often. I was extremely close to Angela and David's children, Stephen and Alan, who were slightly older than Ciara and me. They were almost like brothers to us, and they taught me to love Manchester United (my baby cousin Gary was born when I was about five, and he was an instant friend as well, as would be little Darragh, who came along when I was fourteen). We also saw Uncle Brendan and Auntie Carol a lot. Their children, Lisa and Lavinia, were great pals too, and Ciara and I loved having sleepovers with them. Together with Uncle Paul, Auntie Kelly and their children, Emma, Andrea, Fiona and Gavin; Uncle John, Auntie Linda and their children, Wayne, Avril and Orla; and Uncle Marty, Auntie Bernie and their children, Leona, Brian, Olivia and Sharon, there were always lots and lots of relatives around, and loads of cousins to play with. Mam and Auntie Angela did their big shop together on Thursday nights, and there were also regular visits at the end of the working week. Often on summer weekends, several families would pile into their cars with things to eat and drink and we would all meet up somewhere outdoors to have a picnic lunch – eating sandwiches, crisps and cake until we were as full as a bingo bus, as Mam used to say – so the adults could exchange news and talk while the children played for what seemed like endless hours under a sky that I remember now as being unfailingly blue.

Mam and Dad loved having friends over for dinner. Ciara and I were fed early on those nights – she often had to help me out by sneaking things from my plate when Mam was not looking because I was such a fussy eater and had a very small appetite – and then we were allowed to stay up in our py-jamas to say hello to the guests before we went to bed. As a treat, we would be given some sweets to eat before we brushed our teeth. We were fascinated by the adults' activities, and as soon as we had been tucked in and felt confident that our parents had been distracted by their guests and were not paying any attention to us, we would sneak out of bed and sit on the landing upstairs, listening to the grown-ups' conversation, peeking through the glass panel on the living-room door, and trying to make sense of it.

One of the many things that Ciara and I loved doing when we were very small was rehearsing and putting on little concerts. We both enjoyed singing and dancing, and I absolutely adored doing 'a show'. At Christmas, and on other occasions when the grown-ups gathered downstairs, we got together with our cousins Lisa and Lavinia, raided Mam's dressing table to do our hair and make-up, and put on an entertainment for our parents.

I remember those very early Christmases with some of the wonder that I felt at the time. Santa came, of course. When we woke, we felt the exciting bulk of the full stocking at the end of the bed, and when we crept downstairs we found that he had consumed the mince pie and other things that Ciara and I had left for him and, in exchange, had left us with a huge pile of toys under our brightly decorated Christmas tree. There was always a note: 'Happy Christmas, Marguerite, with love from Santa.'

Uncle David used to organize the Santa at the shopping centre and Ciara and I were allowed to help fill bags with toys to give the children who came to visit. Somehow, we were able to help the volunteer be Santa, while also believing in Santa at the same time. We liked the thought of being Santa's helpers, and imagined how excited the children would be when they got their presents.

Ciara and I remained inseparable as we got older. We still shared a room, shared our friends, and did everything together. Our room had two single beds and lots of space for our toys; I loved my Toby bear, a Christmas present one year, and Ciara was fond of her Monchhichi monkey. One of our favourite toys was a big rag-doll 'golliwog' with elastic bands that you could put under your feet so that you could prance around holding his hands and look as though you were dancing with him. The golliwog was made with black fabric and had big dark eyes and frizzy hair. I really enjoyed playing with my golly. It seems crazy now that most of us have become so aware of racism and how it infiltrates so many aspects of life, but because it did not even look like a human being, none of us Penroses ever realized that the golliwog was supposed to represent a Black man, and that it actually came from a grotesque stereotype with roots in the way Black people were seen and caricatured in a racist America. For us, it was just a friendly toy with a big smile on its soft cloth face, and it reminded us of the dancing cartoon minstrels that advertised Lyon's tea on RTÉ, the Irish national television station. Again, I think hardly anyone knew about the old minstrel shows, when white performers painted their faces black and made fun of Black people. Lyon's tea was a popular brand, so we just associated the minstrels with that. While of course I would never get a golliwog for a child now, as I am aware of the history of the toy, and of the deep, embedded racism of the 'black and white' minstrel shows, I do think that it is unfair to get angry with people who might have bought one in all innocence, as my family did, or in general to judge people in the past by the standards of the present. We will never get anywhere if we waste our outrage and energy on things that have already happened, and that we can no longer do anything about.

There were so many little things that were a constant reminder of the fact that I had come from somewhere else, rather than growing inside Mam, as my sister had done. There were lots of baby photos of Ciara, lovingly document-ing all of her early milestones, but apart from the photo that Mona had given Dad, there were none of me, because I had not met my family yet, and apparently the home had not taken very many. The photographic record of me started at the age of three, as though my parents had gone out into the garden one day and found me under a cabbage. Ciara still had the toys that she had loved when she was a baby, the toys that had always been in her cot, but I had no mementoes from my babyhood at all.

Then there was my hair. Mam had to learn how to deal with my curls, which were not the same as most Irish girls' hair. She bought an Afro comb and learned through trial and error how to use it, and she put conditioner in to make it easier. Because my hair was so difficult to tame it was simpler to wear it short, but when it was very short, I was mistaken for a boy, which I hated. If someone said, 'And who is this lovely little boy?' I would scowl at them furiously. When I was six and a half, Nana Kitty got my ears pierced so that people would not be confused about what sex I was. That made things a little better, but sometimes people did not notice my shiny earrings and still mistook me for a boy, much to my irritation. I longed for a ponytail or a long mane to toss over my shoulders so that I could be more like my sister, who had beautiful long, glossy hair.

When we were seven Ciara and I made our First Holy

Communion together. Mam bought us both beautiful dresses – a short one for me and a long one for Ciara. My dress was lovely, but I wanted to look like my sister, so I kicked up a fuss until Mam arranged to have a second tier of fabric added to mine, because it was too late to get me a new one. As I was so tiny, Mam could not find white Communion shoes in my size, even though she went all over town, and she had to buy me a little pair of black patent leather Mary Janes with a bit of a heel. I remember Nana Josie being horrified that my shoes were black and worried that I would be upset about being the only girl in the class who did not have white shoes, but I was mesmerized by their shininess and by my gorgeous long white dress and did not care. Nana Kitty had bought us matching decorative tulle parasols, and nobody but Ciara and me had them.

The sun shone brightly on the day of our First Holy Communion, and Ciara and I were like princesses. Dressed in our finery, and twirling our parasols madly, we went around to all our relatives to show ourselves off. They all gave us money and we made an absolute fortune. Mam and Dad even took me to St Patrick's to show me to the nuns in my Holy Communion outfit, and they brought me up to Dad's Auntie Molly's so that Molly and Mona, who had initiated the fostering arrangement, could see how pretty I was in my lovely dress. The Communion Mass in the church in Raheny seemed almost like a footnote to the main event, which was the dressing-up and twirling around.

My disability was another big difference between the two of us. Ciara was a tall, strong girl, and I was – and would always be – petite and delicate. Despite the various medical interventions I had experienced in my early years, my spine was curved and my torso jutted a bit to one side above my slender legs, giving me a noticeable limp, although to me it was just the way I was and I never let it hold me back. Mam and Dad's natural instinct was to protect me, but they also knew that they needed to let me push myself, even when it made them anxious. I wanted to do every single thing that Ciara did, from climbing trees to wearing roller skates to playing rough-and-tumble games. Mam and Dad never once told me not to. They explained that some things were more difficult for me than for the other children, and that I should not get upset if I was not always able to do physical things as easily or as quickly as others, but they invariably encouraged me to try and see if there was a way I could do whatever I wanted to, even if I had to do it slightly differently.

Inevitably, because I was the only Black girl in school, the other children could see that I looked different to them, and to the rest of my family, and as we all grew older and they became more aware of the various types of people in the world, they were curious and asked Ciara and me questions.

'But *how* are you sisters?' they would say. 'How are you the same age and different colours?'

Because my parents had always spoken to me and Ciara openly about how I came into the family, I was well equipped with answers, and could explain that I had grown in another mammy's tummy, but that because she could not take care of me, I was with the Penroses now and they were my mammy and daddy instead. It was an easy explanation to understand, and the children accepted it. Most of the time, I was happy to deal with my classmates' questions, but sometimes I would have preferred to talk about something else.

Occasionally when I was out with Mam, an inquisitive adult would come up and start probing me. They were generally friendly, attracted to me because of my unusual appearance.

Sometimes they were interested in the colour of my skin; sometimes they wanted to talk about why I was 'walking like that'; sometimes they were curious about why I was so little, like a curly-headed doll. The term 'body positivity' was not used in those days, and a lot of people felt that they had the right to comment on other people's appearance, just because they felt like it. Most of them were well-meaning, but at times I did not want to deal with their endless questions and would seek refuge behind Mam's legs or look down at my feet, finding it difficult to answer and feeling embarrassed by the unwelcome attention. It made me anxious, because I had been taught to be polite to grown-ups, and I felt that I had to deal with the situation even though I did not want to or know how.

'We'll ask her another time,' Mam would say tactfully, to protect me and to politely tell them to back off and give me some space. 'I don't think she wants to talk about it at the moment.'

4. A Straight Back

As my body grew, and as I wanted to do more and more things, and to throw myself into every activity alongside Ciara and all our friends, my scoliosis was a constant challenge. Because of my condition, I often saw doctors and consultants, and I accepted this as part of my normal life. I knew that, one day, I would have to go into hospital for a 'big operation' that was going to help me grow up straight and taller, like the other girls; and, while I was happy with my life as it was, I looked forward to this. As I approached the age of eight, my doctors felt that I was big enough and mature enough to cope with the surgery and long hospital stay that I would need to have my back straightened in the spinal fusion procedure. It would be difficult, but they were confident of a good outcome.

Mam, Dad and the doctors talked to me about what was going to happen. They explained that it would be tough, and that I would have to stay in hospital for a number of weeks getting better, but it would all be for the best, because when I came out, my back would be straighter, and it would gradually get easier for me to do the things that were harder for me than for other children. I had no idea, then, how major the surgery was, and how risky it would be for me, but I am sure that my parents were under no illusions.

My consultant, Mr Frank Dowling, was the top surgeon for scoliosis in the whole country. He had successfully operated on lots of children, and he was confident that he would be able to help me. I remember him as a tall, well-dressed man with a kind, smiling face and a gentle manner, who always made a point of talking to me as well as to my parents so that I felt cared for and involved in my medical treatment. He chatted to me and asked how I was getting on in school. He was very gifted at talking to his young patients in a way that they could relate to, and at explaining the difficult procedures he carried out in a way that they could understand; I remember him taking out my X-rays and holding them up to the light so that I could see my curved spine while he pointed at the image and described what he was going to do to bring it into line. I saw Mr Dowling so often, I became fond of him, and would look forward to meeting him at my next appointment. He was allowed access to my medical records, but had no information about genetic or other conditions that I might have inherited from my parents.

At the time my life-changing surgery was being organized, I think that I was quite excited at the thought of having a straight back like my sister's, and I know that I trusted Mam, Dad and Mr Dowling and felt certain they were doing what was best for me. They all reassured me and told me that they would be there for me every step of the way. At that young age, I couldn't comprehend how complex the surgery was, and how traumatic the recovery would be – even if everything went perfectly, which was by no means guaranteed.

The hope was that, with my newly straightened spine, I would grow up stronger and with fewer health challenges than otherwise lay ahead. It would be easier for me to breathe because my lungs would no longer be so compressed. It would be easier for me to eat and enjoy a hearty meal, because my stomach would no longer be jostling for position with my other internal organs; Mam had always worried that I was not eating enough, because my stomach had so little space it was not actually physically possible for me to put much food into it. It would be easier for me to run and play, because there would no longer be so much pressure on my pelvis and legs, which had to compensate for my twisted upper body. I would look and feel more like all the other children.

Surgery for scoliosis is always a big intervention, and because my scoliosis was severe, my surgery in Crumlin Children's Hospital was going to be complex. The plan was to place a rod in the base of my spine to fuse it, and then to straighten the curvature in my back. I would need two operations – one to remove bone spurs and other abnormalities, and then another one, which would be a major surgery involving opening my whole back up, to place in the rod. Seven was a good age to carry out the procedure, because I was old enough to understand what was happening, and why, and to submit to the treatment reasonably willingly.

The first surgery, which took about ten hours, seemed to go well, and I remember very little about the two-week recovery period afterwards. At that point, it was time to go in for the second surgery, which would completely change the shape of my back. The nurses smiled at me kindly as they got me ready for the operating theatre, and told me what a brave little girl I was and that they were sure that my mammy and daddy were very proud of me.

'It'll be over before you know it,' they said. 'You won't remember a thing, and when you open your eyes, we will take extra good care of you.'

Afterwards, I was brought to intensive care to start my recovery. I will never forget the time I spent there. Although I was heavily medicated to control the pain, I was conscious and aware of the machines beeping and whirring all around me, of the strong scent of disinfectant in the air, and of the muted comings and goings of the nurses and doctors. There were tubes and wires attached to every part of my body: a catheter taking urine out of my bladder and depositing it into a bag because I could not even use a bedpan; monitors to ensure that my organs were working properly; ports delivering painkilling medication and high doses of antibiotics to stop my wound from getting infected. I was in traction, with bolts screwed into either side of my head and knees to support big metal braces, and my body held firmly in place by weights attached at either end so that, as I healed, I would remain in position.

The surgery that I had just experienced was so major that I was a very sick little girl for a few days. My whole back was covered in a huge dressing that the nurses had to attend to frequently so that an infection would not set in. There were enormous metal staples holding it all together that would have to come out as soon as I was sufficiently healed. I never saw my wounds, but I am sure that they were a horrifying spectacle.

It must have been upsetting and frightening for my parents to see me in that condition, and in that environment, but Mr Dowling told Mam and Dad that the surgery had gone very well and that there was nothing out of the ordinary about my condition in intensive care. The recovery was going to be long and arduous, but he was confident that the outcome would be good, and that I would walk out of the hospital with a straighter back and my head held high. They must have been so relieved; it is extremely upsetting for any parent to see their child in pain and discomfort, and while Mam and Dad never let me see how stressed they were, I know now that it was a very difficult time for them.

We quickly got into a routine. My condition stabilized, so I was discharged from the intensive care unit to a general ward. The nurses took good care of me, and my doctors dropped in to see me frequently. Crumlin Children's Hospital was a teaching hospital, so often the doctors' visits started with a short discussion of who I was and why I was there, in order that the student doctors and nurses accompanying them on their rounds could learn from my case. Most of the doctors went out of their way to speak kindly to their patients, understanding that we were just little children and that we needed extra support and care. Mam was asked, over and over again, to provide details of my medical history because my medical charts did not state that this information was unavailable. Did anyone in my family have diabetes? A history of blood disorders? Disabilities or ailments of any sort? Anything at all of note? Over and over again, she had to tell them that I was her foster child and that, as such, she had no access to medical information about my biological family at all. All of that information belonged to the state, and the state did not think that my parents or doctors needed access to it, even when I was in hospital, recovering from major surgery.

At first, Mr Dowling felt positive about how my recovery was going. He said that I was tougher than I looked, a little fighter, and that I would be up and about in no time.

'Nobody's going to keep Marguerite down,' he said. 'Are they, pet?'

But, about a week after the operation, when I was installed in my own little room beside the nurses' station so that they could keep a close eye on me, Mam noticed that something was wrong. She, Ciara and Gaga had come to visit, bearing a huge pile of get-well cards from all my classmates at school. Face down in my bed, I was looking at the cards, which had been placed underneath me, when Mam realized that I had wet myself without even being aware of it. She asked me to twitch my toes, and although I was sure that I was doing it, my toes did not move at all. Knowing at once that something was wrong, she went to talk to the nurse before going home. After Mam left, the nurse called a doctor, and soon Mr Dowling and a number of other medics were standing around the bed, looking down on me and talking among themselves in rapid, worried tones.

I remember, then, lying in the bed while Mr Dowling leaned over and pulled my blankets up, exposing my ankles and shins to the warm air of the hospital ward. He tapped me on my legs and lower body with a little hammer to see what I could feel. He smiled at me and said that I was being very good.

'Now, Marguerite,' he said. 'Just tell me what you can feel when I do this.'

I could not feel a thing as I was tapped with the tiny hammer, I remember that.

Mr Dowling pulled the blankets back over me and looked at me kindly.

'I'm going to have to have a little chat with your mammy,' he said. 'You've been a great little girl.'

Back at home, Mam had not been able to get rid of the nagging feeling that something was wrong. She rang the hospital, and they confirmed her fears, saying that they were going to take me into surgery first thing in the morning.

I was rushed back to the operating theatre again, and in another procedure lasting about fifteen hours, Mr Dowling removed the rod that he had used to straighten my back just a week before. He hoped that my paralysis would be reversed once the rod was gone.

My parents, of course, dashed to the hospital. When the surgery was over, I was brought to intensive care again, because I was so ill. Mam and Dad were told to prepare themselves for the possibility that things could get even worse. They were informed that, if I survived the night, I would probably be OK, but that my chances of survival at that point were about fifty-fifty. Mam and Dad were scared but they were also hopeful, because they already knew that I was a fighter.

While I was in recovery for the third time, Mr Dowling told my parents that the rod had been removed, but I was still paralysed from the waist down. This was a known, but fairly rare, complication of scoliosis surgery, and I had just been one of the less fortunate ones. This was the first time it had happened to Mr Dowling, and he was absolutely devastated, but it was not his fault. He had checked everything before closing me up, and my spinal column had been pulsating normally. Something had gone wrong. It was just one of those things that could not be explained.

Now I was much worse off than I had been before I came in, and I still had months of recovery ahead of me just to get back to how I had been. Before the surgery, I had been an active, happy little girl who just happened to have curvature of the spine and who never let it stop her from dancing or enjoying her life. Now I was completely dependent on other people, and my spine was as curved as ever.

I was placed in a Stryker bed, which is a special bed that can be flipped around, putting the patient on their back or stomach. At one point, the nurses carefully turned me from my back on to my front, and after a few minutes of staring at the floor I could sense a tickling, sticky feeling on my bare skin. Rivulets of blood were pouring down my sides from the wound on my back. The blood trickled down the bed and dripped on to the polished floor beneath my suspended face, where it pooled and started to congeal. I could smell the metallic odour of my own blood over the sharp scent of the disinfectant that filled the ward. I do not remember if I screamed; I don't know if I was even able to, because I was still very heavily medicated. But I was terrified, and for the first time I had an inkling of what a big operation I had just been through. Afterwards, Mam told me that when she saw the blood pouring down on to the floor she got on her hands and knees and started frantically trying to mop it up, to save me from the trauma of looking at it.

The nurses turned me over every three or four hours all day long, and also all night, so although I was supposed to be resting as much as possible, I never had a full night's sleep. If I needed to use the bathroom, I had to ask a nurse to bring me a bedpan. They were always kind, but I hated doing this because it was uncomfortable and embarrassing, even though they were always very gentle and tried to make me feel at ease. The bedpans were made of stainless steel and were freezing against my bare skin, and they smelled strongly of disinfectant after being washed in the sluice room.

The stress of the situation was absolutely dreadful, but I think the boredom was possibly even worse. As soon as I was well enough to realize how bored I was, I became immensely frustrated. Because of the position I was in, I spent most of my time looking at either the ceiling or the floor. When I was on my back, I could keep an eye on what was going on in the ward by tilting my head, but when I was on my stomach, all I could see was the floor, through a special hole in the bed. There was a mirror to help me see guests, and when I was on my own, the nurses put a book underneath me, and I was able to use my arms rather awkwardly to turn the pages. But most of the time, I just lay there and stared straight ahead, at nothing, wishing that I was at home in the cosy room I shared with my sister and resenting each moment that passed.

Mam came to see me every day, driving the considerable distance from Donaghmede. She would drop Ciara off at school, spend as much time as possible with me, and then get back for three to pick Ciara up again. While I was obviously in need of a lot of special attention and care, it was also important to make sure that Ciara's needs were being met. Dad did not drive in those days, so when he came, it took even longer, because he was on the bus. Whenever he could, he caught two or three buses to get to Crumlin Hospital to visit me in the evenings after work. At weekends, different relatives would pop in to see how I was doing, and Ciara would come in to chat to me and cheer me up. My family's visits reminded me that I was loved and that I had a wonderful life outside the hospital.

I remember only one day when, for some reason, Mam was unable to visit. Accustomed as I was to seeing her every day, I was absolutely distraught. I cried and cried and, even though the nurses did their best to comfort me, I got into such a state that they were worried I would make myself sick. There were no mobile phones in those days, so they wheeled my Stryker bed to the family room, where there was a telephone attached to the wall. The telephone receiver on its long curly wire was stretched over to me so that I could talk to Mam and hear her voice on the other end of the line. When she answered, I went into hysterics.

'Take me home, Mam!' I screamed, clutching the receiver as hard as I could, as though by pressing it into my hands I was actually touching Mam. 'Take me home! Don't leave me here! I want to come home! I don't want to be here any more!'

Somehow poor Mam eventually managed to calm me down and the nurses brought me back to the ward, still crying and protesting that I wanted my mother and that I wanted to leave.

Children are very resilient, and they learn to make the best of whatever situation they are in. As the weeks turned into months, I got to know the doctors and nurses very well. They were all extremely kind to me. Mr Dowling dropped by to see me and say hello every time he visited the ward, even if I was not on his schedule. The other doctors and nurses always made time to have a little chat. They all did their best to keep me company and brought me packets of Manhattan peanuts when they came back from being on a break because they knew that I liked them. Finding it so difficult to sleep, I often spent half the night awake and talking to the medical staff. I got to know everyone who came to the ward. The cleaners, who visited every day to polish the shiny floors, clean the glass dividers between each room, and change bedlinen, went out of their way to talk to me too, even though they were so busy.

Despite the multiple kindnesses of everyone at the hospital, and their efforts to make the children as happy as possible, I still cried bitter tears every time my parents came to visit, demanding that they take me home there and then. I could not understand why they had to leave me there, when all I wanted was to be at home. I felt that I had been abandoned in the hospital and, even though I understood when it was explained to me why I had to stay for now, the moment I saw my family members getting ready to leave, I would work myself up into a frenzy, feeling that they were all going off to have a nice time without me, and that it was not fair that I was being left behind.

St Catherine's Ward on the top floor of Crumlin Hospital was my home for months. It was subdivided into many little rooms, but so that the nurse in charge could see what was going on in each one, the walls were made of glass. Most of the other children there had severe illnesses, such as leukaemia and other types of childhood cancer. There were a lot of children with cystic fibrosis, many of whom were very seriously ill. They were all as miserable as I was. Some of them were babies or toddlers, too young to understand why they were in hospital, and utterly traumatized by having apparently been abandoned by their parents. The sick children were from all over the country, so often their parents could only visit once in a while, as they lived elsewhere and had jobs they needed to do and other children to take care of. I can still remember the faces of those desperately unwell children looking back at me from their glass-panelled rooms and hearing their cries as their parents had to leave them after visiting.

When a child got well enough to go home, there was always a festive atmosphere as their delighted parents collected them and they said goodbye to the other little patients. Once in a while a child just disappeared and the rest of us did not know where they had gone. Presumably, they had passed away, and the other children were not told what had happened.

Because Mam and Dad were visiting me all the time, and because I was in hospital for so long, they soon knew not just the doctors and nurses, but also all the other children on the ward. They used to come in with sweets in their pockets and go around to have a little chat with everyone, not just me.

They tried to make things more fun for me by wheeling me around in my Stryker bed so that I could visit the other kids and say hello.

It is only now, as an adult, that I can begin to understand how difficult that time must have been for my parents. Then, I had no hint of it, because they were always positive and smiling. Dad says that, while he already knew that he loved me before I went in for the surgery, the terrible emotional pain that the whole situation caused him was confirmation that I really was his little girl, because he hurt just as badly as he would have done if I had been his biological child.

Once in a while I was wheeled down to the next floor for an X-ray. The floor below was a complete mystery to me, as St Catherine's Ward was my whole world in hospital. Not only were the patients different on the next floor, all the doctors and nurses were different too. I remember waiting on several occasions for an X-ray, looking at the unfamiliar faces passing by. On this floor, there were often parents in floods of tears, crying and holding on to one another, totally beside themselves. Nobody ever explained to me what was going on down there, but it must have been a place where only very seriously ill children were treated, and I suppose that many of them never got better. I can still remember those parents' cries and how they echoed in the corridor, the sounds of their anguish amplified by all the hard, shiny surfaces, while the doctors, nurses and cleaning staff rushed by them unresponsively – not because they did not care, but just because they were so busy and, I suppose, because the sounds of grief had become so familiar that they were simply part of the background noise.

Because I had been given so many injections, and had so much blood taken for testing, I had learned to dread the arrival of any sort of needle. Every so often I would see a nurse on her way to draw someone's blood – they always carried a distinctive box, like a fishing tackle box, to do that – and I would go crazy, crying hysterically. If Mam was there, she would try to comfort me.

'They're not even coming to you!' she would say. 'Hush, now. Everything is fine.'

Once in a while they were coming for me, though, and then I had to be calmed down before anything could be done. When it actually happened, it was never as bad as I thought it was going to be. The anticipation of pain was by far the worst part of the ordeal.

That year, 1981, the Eurovision Song Contest was held in Dublin, because Johnny Logan had won it for Ireland the year before. A day or two after the competition, the winning act, Bucks Fizz, came to visit the Children's Hospital to meet the kids and pose for photographs with them. The wards were all abuzz as they did the rounds, accompanied by hordes of television reporters and cameramen. They all signed a copy of their album and gave it to me; I was absolutely thrilled. That evening I was featured on the news on RTÉ, meeting Bucks Fizz from my Stryker bed.

Mam had taken Ciara out of school early and rushed to the hospital in the hope that she would be able to see Bucks Fizz too. The singers had gone by the time Mam and Ciara got there, but the children's beds were still in the corridors, where they had been brought to see the performers. Mam wheeled me back to the ward, but when we got there, the staff were cleaning my room, and we had to wait outside for a while. Mam lifted the sheet covering my legs and told me to twitch my toes; she did this every time she came in, and every time I thought I was doing what she told me, but my toes had always remained completely still. That day, however, for the first time since my surgery, one of my toes moved, just a little. Shortly afterwards, Mr Dowling and his team came to examine me, and said that the twitching toe was a good sign. While there was still no guarantee that I would walk again, there was hope that perhaps things would get better.

To give me back as much movement as possible, I had to do physiotherapy several times a day. I absolutely hated it, and was not very cooperative. The physiotherapist did her best to be kind, but it hurt to do the things she asked of me, and I was angry and distressed. I cried furiously, refused to do what she was telling me was so important for my recovery, and made things very difficult for her. She tried to make me use supportive bars to hold my body up by my arms and coax my legs to move. The feeling had begun to return to my lower body, but I was still unable to move my legs, which just dangled there uselessly while my arms ached from the effort of pulling. It hurt so much, and was so frustrating, that to this day when I see bars like that, I feel physically sick.

I had been so unwell at Christmas that I have no memory of spending it in hospital. I have only the vaguest recollection of turning eight that January. But as the days started getting longer, I grew a little stronger and more able to take an interest in things. Easter came and went. I was given so many chocolate Easter eggs that year that Mam had to take most of them home, promising that she would keep them safe for me to enjoy when I got out.

'It won't be long now, pet,' Mam said. 'I talked to Mr Dowling and he said that you can come home soon.'

Months after my initial surgery, I was still in hospital, still unable to walk although I was now able to twitch my toes, and desperately unhappy. This had been an extremely challenging time for my parents too. Eventually, Mam went to the doctors and said, 'What's going to happen now? She can't stay in hospital for the rest of her life.'

For months, Mam had had to live not just with seeing me go through three major surgeries and all the pain that went with them; she had also had to come to terms with the fact that the procedures had failed, and that I was now worse off than I had been before. Every time she left, she had to unpeel my arms from her, watch my face crumple into tears, and hear my cries as she said goodbye and walked down the corridor away from me and towards the lift. I cannot imagine how she coped.

'We can't keep putting Marguerite through this,' Mam told the medical staff. 'It's just not fair. She's been in hospital for months, and she deserves to be at home with her family. She deserves some semblance of a normal life. She's just a child.'

Everyone could see that it was not doing me any good to stay in hospital long-term, so my medical team started working towards making me less dependent on their care. The first step was getting me out of my Stryker bed and into a normal bed and a wheelchair that could be used to bring me about and facilitate my interactions with others. My spine was so weak and compromised that I needed a plaster of Paris vest to hold me upright as it continued to heal, with a view to my becoming strong enough to go home again.

The day that the plaster of Paris cast was put around my upper torso was a very happy one. I was so thrilled at the prospect of finally being able to sit up and look around, rather than just lying flat on my bed, staring at the ceiling or the floor. A whole team of doctors had to carefully hold my body in place while the cast went on. The plaster felt rough against my skin, but as it hardened, I began to feel how it was holding me up. There was a lot of discussion about how to smooth the edges of the armholes so that they would be reasonably comfortable. Eventually, the medical team propped me up and, for the first time in months, I could look my doctors and my family in the face from the pillows helping me to sit upright in bed, and my parents were able to take me out of the main hospital in my wheelchair and walk around the grounds, so that I could see the sky and feel the fresh air against my skin.

Soon, I could use the wheelchair on my own and even wheel myself around – up and down the shiny, polished floor of the hospital ward and in and out of the other children's rooms. Now, when my parents came to visit, they could take me to the hospital canteen and the little shop downstairs for a treat. As I got strong enough, I started to wheel myself down to the lift to say goodbye when Mam was leaving. She would get in and I would watch as the steel doors closed over that beloved face. My finger would dash out and press the 'open doors' button to reveal Mam standing there, in her coat, ready to go. I would do this over and over again. We would both laugh, pretending that it was a game, pretending that we were having fun. Eventually Mam would say that she really did need to go home now, and I would stop pressing the button and just sit there, all alone in my wheelchair, listening to the whine of the lift carrying Mam downstairs and away from me.

I was supposed to be strapped into the wheelchair to keep me from falling out, but I hated the constraints because they seemed like yet another obstacle in my path. One day I made a huge fuss about the straps, saying that I did not need them and would be perfectly fine without them. The nurses let me go off without being secured, and of course when someone wheeled me up the corridor, I fell forwards. The weight of the cast made me crash heavily to the floor, where I landed on my face. The doctors had to check me over, and Mam had to be told what had happened, but fortunately I had no serious injuries. I never complained about having to be strapped in again.

All of the children who were in Crumlin Hospital long-term were supposed to go to school, so in the mornings lessons were held for us, and I was brought down in my wheelchair. The teacher did her best with a large group of sick and traumatized children of varying ages, but it was extremely difficult for her to manage, as we were all feeling unwell and were all in different classes on the outside. I hated school in the hospital and was almost always too tired to even listen to the teacher, because I rarely slept well and had often been up half the night talking to the doctors. I was usually sleeping when the catering staff brought around breakfast, and often woke up with a sausage on a fork clutched in my hand, where they had helpfully placed it.

To avoid going to school, I soon learned how to pretend I was asleep in the morning when the staff came by to collect the children and bring them down to class, opening one eye when I heard the door close behind the other kids on their way out. Because I had been in hospital so long, and knew the staff so well, they were very indulgent of me, and I actually attended school very rarely.

After many months in hospital, my progress had plateaued. While the multiple scars on my back had healed, apart from twitching my toes a little, I was still completely unable to move anything below my waist. I continued to loathe physiotherapy, and remained very resistant to doing the exercises that were supposed to give me a chance of getting out of my wheelchair one day. Mam and Dad could see that my mental well-being was suffering, while my physical health was not improving, so they talked things over with Mr Dowling, and agreed with him that I would be discharged from hospital and allowed to go home as soon as possible. At first, I would just be going home for a day, then the weekends, to see how I got on. Then if things went well, I would be allowed to stay with them for longer, until the wonderful day when I did not need to go back to hospital at all. It was just like when I first met the Penroses, and was being integrated into the family. This approach would also give Mam and Dad the chance to learn how to do my physiotherapy with me so that they could treat me at home themselves in the hope that my condition would improve over time.

I had walked into the children's hospital on my own two feet, and now I was going to go home in a wheelchair, with the doctors having told my parents that I might never walk again. The doctors and my parents explained the whole situation to me as clearly as they could: that the surgery had not worked out as we had all hoped, so I would be going home with a curve in my back still, and that now I also had to try my very best to learn how to walk again as I was still paralysed, and would have to be a brave girl and work hard to do all my exercises, even though I hated them. I nodded and said that I understood – and to some extent I did – but all I could focus on was the fact that, at long last, I was about to start going home to our cosy house, my loving parents, my beloved sister Ciara, our red setter Mandy, and my many toys and books.

Children who are sick, and in particular children who are born sick, generally grow up to be very tough, as I have done. Because we have had to face so many challenges, and have overcome them, we are unafraid. I was already a resilient little girl before I had the surgery, but my experiences in Crumlin changed my life in many ways, some of which I am only now beginning to fully understand.

I think that a prolonged period in hospital will change anyone for ever. A child, going through it at a sensitive time in their development, will keep the memory with them all their life. I know that my long stay at Crumlin Children's Hospital was instrumental in making me the person I am today. Even now, all these years later, I can hardly bear to watch TV shows set in hospitals. The beeping of the monitors triggers painful memories that I do my best not to think about, and I find myself getting upset. I hate to see or smell blood, as it reminds me of my surgeries, of the many blood samples I gave, and of the children who came on to my ward for treatment, like me, but who never made it home. I have learned, over the years, to tolerate injections and my blood being drawn for tests, because I know how important it is, but I still find it difficult.

What I went through as a child was no one's fault, but it was one of the biggest traumas that I have ever endured. It was awful, but I know that it has made me very tough. I am still petite, and I still have severe scoliosis, and it is easy for people to underestimate me or to assume that I am weak and need a lot of help. But anyone who knows me well knows that I can put up with anything and come out the other side with a smile on my face. My childhood experience in hospital taught me that, no matter how bad things are, there is no choice but to plough through them. That you just have to be strong and determined if you are going to get to the other side.

Sometimes my deep reservoir of emotional strength can make me a little impatient with people who complain about what seem to me to be small problems that should not really matter. Crossly, I think to myself, Well, good for you, if *that's* the worst thing that's ever happened to you!

I am not proud of reacting like that, however, because I know it is not fair. Mostly, I do my best to channel my toughness into being as active and busy as possible, into filling my life and living it to the full, because I know how fragile happiness can be, and how easily it can be taken away.

I know that I am very blessed to have a wonderful family, lots of friends, and to live in a wealthy, privileged country. I know that there are countless people who are infinitely worse off than I am. And, because I am the tough one, because I am a survivor, I also believe that I have a responsibility to do whatever I can to make things easier for them.

5. She May Never Walk Again

I remember the first day home as if it was yesterday. I was so delighted. Mam collected me at the hospital and brought me home with my wheelchair, which could be folded so as to fit into the car. The wheelchair was very heavy and quite awkward, but Mam managed to deal with it on her own, and both Mam and Dad would become experts at dealing with it over the weeks and months that followed.

'Let's go and see Dad at work,' Mam said. 'He'll be so excited.'

Ciara got her bicycle and rode alongside my wheelchair as we started out on the ten-minute walk. It was a beautiful sunny day, and the housing estate was looking glorious, with flowers in all the front gardens and children playing outside their houses and on the streets. It took us about two hours to walk the short distance from our house to the shopping centre, because every neighbour that we passed rushed out to see me, tell me that they had missed me, and ask Mam how I was getting on.

'It's wonderful to have you back, Marguerite,' they all said.

My face hurt from smiling so much.

Children who had grown since I saw them last stared at my wheelchair, their eyes wide in amazement, as most of them had never seen one before.

'You can touch it if you want,' I said, pleased and a little proud to see that my wheelchair was now the centre of such positive attention.

My friend Yvonne lived halfway between our house and the shopping centre where Dad worked, so we stopped at her road, where we knew everyone too. Once again, they all came out to see me, praise me, and tell me how happy they were that I was back.

When we got to the shopping centre, Mam brought me into Uncle David's electrical shop. As she pushed me in, Dad and Uncle David's faces turned towards me, lit by huge, wonderful smiles.

'There's my special girl!' Dad said. 'Back with us at last.'

Then, while Mam and Uncle David chatted, Dad wheeled me around the shopping centre so that I could say hello to all the people working in the shops, most of whom had known me since I was little. All these months, they had been asking Dad how I was, wishing me well, and lighting candles for me in church. I am sure that they were disappointed to see me in a wheelchair instead of running around with a newly straightened back, but none of them let their pity show on their faces. They all pressed money into my hand – 'a little present for a gorgeous girl on her big day' – and I was brought to my favourite shop upstairs, the bookshop, to buy myself a present. I felt like royalty.

Back at home, Mam got out the Easter eggs that I had not been able to eat in hospital and we had a party on the street and shared them with all the other children. Soon all the children were on a sugar high, chocolate smeared around their mouths, running, jumping, and wild with excitement. Stuck in my wheelchair, I could not join them, but I was so thrilled to be home for the day, sharing my chocolate with all my friends, I did not even care.

While it was painful going back to the hospital after that magical day, now that I knew I would soon be home for ever, things got a little easier. I started coming home for whole weekends, and before too long, after nine months in hospital, I was discharged into my parents' care, and my ordeal was over at last. Before leaving for good, I was brought on a triumphant tour of the wards to say goodbye to all the nurses and doctors. They had all been very kind to me, but I still could not wait to get out of there and never have to see any of them again.

Mam and Dad had to use my wheelchair to bring me anywhere, and they also had to carry me quite a lot, as fewer places were wheelchair-friendly in those days than they are now. They had been warned that I might never walk again, but they were determined to give me the best chance possible and, even though I remained very cross and uncooperative about the exercises I was supposed to do, they made sure that I did them. As well as the exercise routine that she had been taught by the hospital, every day Mam got me to stand up and helped me to take a few steps. The fact that I was so small and light was helpful, as she was able to support me while I protested, groaned, whined, and eventually tried to do what she was asking of me.

That summer, we went to Clare on our holidays together with Auntie Angela and Uncle David, and our cousins, Stephen, Alan and Gary, who were close enough in age to Ciara and me to be excellent playmates for us. I am sure that every instinct in their bodies was telling Mam and Dad to protect me and keep me safe – and they did, of course; but they also made sure that the holiday was an exciting adventure for me, as it was for the rest of the children. No big mystery was made of the wheelchair, which was soon integrated into our games, with the kids taking turns having wheelchair races up and down the garden of our rented cottage, my cousins pushing me about and giving me wheelies. Our family albums from that year show me 'paddling' in my wheelchair in the shallow waves on the beach, and playing with shells and building sandcastles with my sister and my cousins, the wheelchair in the background, covered in sand. I even got to ride a pony, just like the other kids, with my parents holding me up on either side. As always, Mam and Dad's priority was for me to have a full, happy childhood. They had hoped that, by now, my back would be straight and fully healed, and that I would be able to run and jump as quickly as the other children. It must have been painful for them to realize that that was not to be, but they never let me see their disappointment, and I remember those long summer days as very joyful ones.

Mam and Dad were anxious for me to get back to a normal life as quickly as possible, so they arranged for me to start school that September, wheelchair or not. As I had effectively missed a whole year, I was kept back to repeat second class. Ciara stayed back too, as we had always been in the same year. We would both have hated it if she had gone ahead. My teacher that year was Miss Emerson, and she was kind and welcoming when I reappeared after my long time away.

The other children in the class were fascinated by my wheelchair; it was like turning up in school with a shiny new bike.

'Can I have a go?' I was often begged. 'Please?'

All the other girls wanted to 'have a go', so when school was on a lunch break I often agreed to be lifted out and parked somewhere so that they could get in and be wheeled up and down, arguing about whose turn it was next. Ciara was tall and strong and knew how to lift me, so she generally

71

did the honours. Other times, one of the girls would dump her school bag in my lap and wheel me triumphantly around the yard as though I was a little empress, the two of us having a brilliant time. I was definitely singled out for being in a wheelchair, but I did not mind at all being the centre of attention, and liked the fact that the other girls were excited and impressed by it and saw it as a sort of toy rather than a barrier between us.

While Mam and Dad were not religious, my two grandmothers shared a devout faith, and they had both been praying hard for me the whole time I was in hospital. Nana Kitty was a member of a women's religious organization, and when her friends heard that I was home, but wheelchair-bound, they did a collection for me and offered to bring me on an all-expenses-paid trip to Lourdes, France. Lourdes has been a major destination for the ill, the disabled and those who love them since the mid-nineteenth century, and Nana Kitty's friends were delighted to be going on pilgrimage, bringing sick and disabled children to the shrine in the hope that there would be a miracle, or at least some spiritual relief from the suffering that they and their families were going through. Nana Kitty discussed the opportunity of going to Lourdes with Mam, who did not expect a miracle to take place, but did think that it would be good for me to get away and do something special – remember that international travel was much more expensive in those days, so going abroad was more of a treat than it is today.

From my perspective, the trip to Lourdes was incredible fun from the moment Nana Kitty, Mam and I arrived at the airport. All the older ladies on the pilgrimage were themselves wildly excited about being overseas, some of them for the first time ever. Most of them spent their lives looking after everyone else in their families and now, for one precious week, they did not have to prepare a single meal or run the Hoover around a single room, because it was all being taken care of by the hotel staff. At the hotel, the ladies scurried from one bedroom to another to enjoy cups of tea, biscuits and even – amid gales of laughter – small glasses of sherry, perched on beds or bedside lockers. Those ladies may have come for the prayers, but they were determined to have a good time while they were at it. Together with Nana Kitty and her friends, Mam and I went to Mass, said the rosary and visited the shrine, but mostly I remember all those grannies away from their many responsibilities just enjoying one another's company and having the time of their lives.

Nana Kitty had sincerely hoped that there would be a miracle for me in Lourdes. That I would be one of the lucky few to arise and walk after being dipped in the holy water at the grotto. While Mam had spoken to me quietly about this, explaining that we were not going in the expectation that I would suddenly get better, but to keep Nana Kitty company, see Lourdes and pray a little, deep down a small part of me thought about what Nana Kitty had told me, and wondered if I might have a miracle after all. What if I was one of God's chosen ones, and was able to step right out of my wheelchair after visiting the shrine at Lourdes? What if I was even luckier than that, and my silly back just straightened itself out? Wouldn't it be amazing if I walked down the steps of the plane when we landed in Dublin? Wouldn't Ciara be so happy that I could run and play with her again, after all these months?

If Nana Kitty was disappointed when there was no miracle for me at Lourdes, she did not lose her faith in the power of prayer. Back home, she was determined to get Padre Pio's glove for me, in the hope that it would make a difference. Padre Pio was an Italian priest and mystic who died in the 1960s. On his hands he had wounds – stigmata – that mysteriously bled at the very spots where Jesus had been crucified. He was still very popular in those days and a lot of people had huge faith in his relics. Most of the relics were cloths or other items that had been in contact with his stigmata and still bore traces of his blood. The glove, which was held in Ireland and was considered a particularly powerful relic, was a fingerless mitten that the great man had worn when he displayed his bleeding stigmata to the adoring crowds that flocked to attend his audiences. It was perennially in huge demand around Dublin, as many people believed that being near the glove could bring about a miracle, and there were always hundreds of people in need of special help.

I do not know what strings Nana Kitty managed to pull, but we had the glove for several days, and for three or four nights I slept with it in my room. Having the glove was a huge deal, and for as long as it was in the house, I felt like an absolute celebrity, because all the neighbours came to take a look at it and to offer their hope that I would be miraculously cured.

I never did experience a miracle in the way that Nana Kitty hoped. No hand from heaven picked me up out of my wheelchair and held me upright, the water at Lourdes was simply wet and cold, Padre Pio's glove could not help, and while hundreds of candles were lit for me, and hundreds of prayers offered up, the injuries that my failed surgery had inflicted continued to prevent me from walking.

But then, one day, while I was doing the exercises that I hated so much, something happened. All of a sudden, to my surprise as much as Mam's, I found that I was able to put one foot in front of the other by myself for the first time since my surgery. I took three small steps across the dining room towards her before collapsing in a heap.

'Oh my God!' Mam shrieked. 'You did it! You walked, Marguerite!'

As soon as I was settled comfortably, Mam told everyone what I had done. Much as I had resented the exercises that she had made me do every day for months, I could hardly contain my excitement as everyone came to congratulate me on my achievement.

After that, little by little, I started to walk, first slowly and unsurely, and then a bit more confidently. Gradually, as I became steadier on my feet, and as my battered muscles started to regain strength after all the months of immobility, I became less dependent on my wheelchair and the help of others. Eventually, my plaster cast came off. While I had not thought that I minded being the only girl in school who had to use a wheelchair, when I was finally able to leave it at home and make it through the school day by myself, I was thrilled. I was even able to join in Miss Dickson's Irish dancing classes, hopping around with the other girls to the very best of my ability. My strength built until I could go outside and play with the other children again, and eventually, about a year and a half after leaving hospital, I was dancing and skipping as I had always done – but now with a back riddled with scars and nine months' worth of hospital memories to process, along with the knowledge that my scoliosis was for ever and that I would never be just like the other little girls.

In a way, I did experience a miracle, although not the sort that Nana Kitty had hoped and prayed for. My miracle was my parents' faith in me, their persistence in doing exercises with me even though I often kicked off and refused to cooperate, and their belief that if I was given the help and support I needed, I would walk again.

The even bigger miracle was that, six years earlier, the Penroses had taken me out of the institution where I had been born, and had brought me into their home and their hearts. If I had remained in state care, and had been undergoing rehabilitation after a failed surgery there, I doubt that anyone would have had the time to put me through all the physiotherapy that Mam did with me every day. I would not have recovered the use of my legs, and – if still alive at all – I would be in a wheelchair.

Most children who undergo treatment for scoliosis have an excellent outcome and, in the developed world where these surgeries have become commonplace, almost all of them grow up with straight backs and without the host of problems that often go hand in hand with the disability. Unfortunately for me, surgery made the situation worse, not better. But I know that the outcome I experienced was nobody's fault; I was given the best treatment available and it was, as Mr Dowling said at the time, just one of those things.

I would continue to see Mr Dowling over the years after my surgery, and he remained as kind and gentle as he had always been. While he was never anything but professional with me, I appreciate that it was painful for him to see me and know that his efforts had failed.

'You're the one who turned my hair grey,' he used to say ruefully. 'I've had a lot of sleepless nights over you, Marguerite.'

In fact, his hair, which had been dark when I met him, was indeed turning grey only a year or two later. Maybe it was just a coincidence, but I am sure that it was very hard for a successful, accomplished and compassionate doctor to look at his little patient and know that, not only had his intervention failed to help, but it had actually made things worse. I had been the only one of the many young patients Mr Dowling had treated whose surgery had been a complete failure. He must have looked at me and known that my back was covered in scars that would never go away, that will always be a reminder of everything I endured to no end as a child. That I would never grow up straight and strong, as my medical team had hoped. That, rather than walking and moving more easily, I would always have problems with walking and balance – more so than before the surgery, rather than less. That my future would be different to the one that he had imagined for me. That I would always have a disability.

On hearing my story, people often ask if my parents were angry with the doctors whose treatment did not work, if they sued the hospital, and if I received a payout to compensate me for the months of pain and poor outcome of my surgery. The truth is that my family never considered suing anyone, not even for a moment. They had known from the outset that there was a risk, and understood that it was just unfortunate that things had not worked out for me the way everyone hoped they would. I had been their little girl before the surgery, and I was still their little girl afterwards. Of course, they were disappointed for me, but we all worked together to stay positive and remain focused on the future.

Back then, I did not fully understand the implications of the fact that everything had gone wrong for me. I was just so happy to be back home with my family. As I grew up, I would gradually come to appreciate how much I would have gained, if my spine had been successfully straightened. Because I have always had so much support from the people around me, I have been able to come to terms with and accept the situation as it is. But, of course, I have my regrets.

Not many people would actively choose to have a disability and, if I could, I would love to be rid of the health issues that I have lived with all my life. Nonetheless, I also know that most disabled people can have rich and fulfilling lives if they have support. Notwithstanding the physical limitations that I have, and that have impacted on my life in so many ways, I have never let my disability hold me back, and even struggle to think of myself as disabled or to claim that label for myself, as I have such a full and active life, when there are others who are so much less fortunate than me. My body is what it is, and I have to love it, because it is the only one I will ever get.

A lot of people who live with disabilities have extremely positive personalities and outlooks on life. People who do not know what it is like to live with physical challenges must sometimes wonder how and why. But just think of the alternative. How horrible it would be to constantly feel angry or bitter about having a disability. How much better it is to accept reality, live with it, and have a wonderful life.

Surgical techniques and medical technology have advanced a great deal since I was a child. Now the doctors treating scoliosis can test their patients during surgery to make sure that there is no paralysis as a result of the intervention, avoiding the bad outcome that I experienced. Success rates for this sort of surgery are very high, and they are getting better all the time. But, despite all this progress, in Ireland today there are still lots of children on waiting lists for the scoliosis surgery that will change their lives for the better. Some of them wait for years; I have met one woman whose little grandson had to suffer so long that the bones of his tortured spine actually started to come out through his skin. It is shocking to think that, even though we live in a wealthy

78

country, we cannot treat some of our most vulnerable citizens when they need it.

As an adult, I have explored whether surgery is still an option for me, but given the huge risks involved in operating on an adult spine, no doctor would recommend such a step, and while my health needs can be complex still, I have a good life that has been largely uncompromised by the physical challenges I live with. Whenever I can, I try to encourage other people who are learning how to walk again after an accident or injury, or who are coming to terms with the limits that their bodies place on them. I know from experience that we are all much stronger than we think.

In my day, we all had to come to terms with the fact that I was going to grow up with the scoliosis I was born with. I think that this was probably easier for me than it was for my parents. While my time in hospital, and the recovery afterwards, was extremely traumatic, I bounced back and, as I grew bigger, I was very excited about what the future held and felt that I was ready for whatever was thrown at me. I would not say that I was left without emotional scars – as well as physical ones – after my failed surgery, but I did rebound quickly in most ways, helped by my large, loving family, and the resilience that I had shown since I was little. As soon as I was home, I relegated my long hospitalization firmly to the past and immersed myself in the important task of getting on with the rest of my life.

Feeling that it would be good for me to get out and mix with other children in a structured setting, especially after all that I had missed during my time in hospital, Mam enrolled Ciara and me in the local chapter of the Brigín Guides, which is the younger division of the Catholic Girl Guides of Ireland. She got us all kitted out with our uniforms and we attended a few meetings, but neither of us liked it and gradually we stopped going. After all that I had been through, Mam was never going to make me continue with something I didn't enjoy.

Around this time, Mam had to bring me to the dentist for my regular check-up. He tilted me back in the chair and peered into my mouth.

'Hmm,' he said as he examined my teeth. 'Well, it looks like this young lady is going to need braces.'

The dentist started explaining to Mam that he was going to suggest a special brace for me that I would have to wear on the outside of my face, as well as inside my mouth. It would be a sort of metal frame that would put pressure on my teeth and get them to grow in a certain way; much bigger and more cumbersome than the braces that kids have today.

'I'll stop you right there,' Mam said icily, while he was in full flow. 'I'm not going to put my daughter through all that so soon after spending nearly a year in hospital and just after she's given up using her wheelchair.'

Seeing that Mam meant business, the dentist finished the consultation quickly, and we went home. Mam was still irritated with him when we got back to the house and I heard her telling people that she had had to stand up for me, that the dentist had had the nerve to suggest yet another medical intervention for a little girl who had already dealt with more in her short life than most people do in a lifetime.

Looking back, I feel a bit sorry for the dentist. After all, he was just doing his job, and it was not his fault that I had spent so long in hospital being treated for something else. But I can also see that his suggestion about the braces had triggered a very deep upset in Mam, who had worked so hard all the time I was in hospital, and during my lengthy recovery, to always be positive, to always have a smile, to never let me see that my ordeals were difficult for her too. As an adult now, I can imagine how traumatic that period must have been for her, and how hard it must sometimes have been never to let her distress show. Despite not having the full brace the dentist wanted me to wear, my adult teeth ended up perfectly straight anyway, so Mam was right.

6. A Big Girl Now

By the time I was confident on my feet again, the long stay I had endured in hospital seemed to fade into the background. Ciara and I made our way through primary school and I thought less and less about the months I had spent away from my family. But an ongoing source of irritation to me were the visits of my social worker, a kind lady called Mairéad, who continued to come to see me every six months or so, as she had done before I went to hospital, for as long as I could remember.

Mairéad never stayed for more than an hour or so. She would sit in the kitchen with Mam, drink tea, and ask her boring questions about how I was getting on at school, and if I was eating well; I had always been a very fussy eater. When Mam had answered all her questions, then she would talk to me on my own about how I was. We only ever spoke for a few minutes at a time. She was perfectly pleasant to me, and I did my best to chat to her in a friendly fashion because I could see that she was trying to be nice. Still, Mairéad's presence felt like a violent intrusion into my life and an unwelcome reminder of the fact that I had not always been with the Penroses and that – at least in theory – someone might take me away from them one day.

Now, looking back, I can understand that, as I was in foster care and officially a ward of state, obviously the authorities had to make sure that I was OK – in earlier generations none of these safety measures were taken, often with catastrophic results – but as a child I hated every minute of Mairéad's visits and would watch the clock on the wall, willing her to go away and resenting all of her kindly-put questions. It had been bad enough that I had been removed from my family to spend nine months in hospital for surgery that had not even worked, and still I had to put up with this woman, with her official-looking clipboard, reminding me that I was not Mam and Dad's real daughter, or at least not in the same way that Ciara was. Ciara looked just like Mam at the same age, everyone said so, and I did not look like any of my relatives at all.

At the back of my mind, I worried that one day my biological mother might suddenly reappear and want me after all, and that I would have to go to live with someone I had no memory of ever meeting. There were lots of films on TV and stories in books about children who finally met their biological parents, having been separated from them for one reason or another. Usually those stories had endings that were supposed to be happy, involving the children having a lovely new life, back with the mother or father who loved them, but the last thing that I wanted was to be taken away from the Penroses and our enchanted existence in Donaghmede. I think that a little part of me feared that, one day, Mairéad would appear with this unwelcome news and would wait downstairs while I was sent up to the bedroom I shared with my sister to pack my clothes and toys before saying goodbye to the only family that I could remember.

When Mairéad left, Mam and I would both say goodbye very politely and then smile at each other in relief as the door closed behind her and she walked down the garden path to her car. I would watch her drive off, and feel my body physically relax once she was out of sight. As soon as Mairéad was gone, order was restored to our home, everything was as it should be, and I could return to my life in the knowledge that I was with the family that I belonged to, tied to them by love rather than biology.

Ciara and I were very popular with the other children at school and in our neighbourhood, partly because Dad's job meant that we always had all the latest gadgets at home. We had a video player and recorder before anyone else. We had electric sandwich toasters and a microwave before anyone else, the best record and cassette players, and all the 1980s technology you could imagine. All the kids we knew wanted to come to our house to look at all these cool things and try them out. They also loved playing at ours because they were almost never asked to be quiet or to tone it down.

Unlike mothers who needed a bit of space and some peace and quiet, Mam absolutely loved it when the house was filled with squealing children. She always told Ciara and me not to leave anyone out and not to treat any of the children on the street less favourably than the others.

'One in, all in,' Mam said firmly. 'That's the rule in this house. Nobody gets left out.'

That meant that if we invited one child from the street to play, we invited all of them. So our house was often filled with the joyful noise of lots of kids and Mam spent loads of time wiping off sticky fingermarks and plying us with tall glasses of MiWadi and slices of cake, all of which she did with a smile. If we had a birthday party, the whole class had to come, and then stay for hours until the last treat was gone and the house had been turned upside down by an excited horde of children. Birthday parties were a huge production, with jelly, ice cream, Rice Krispie buns, home-made birthday cake, and party hats for all the guests. Our house was the party-house, and Ciara and I loved it and basked in the envy of our friends.

While Ciara and I were often busy playing with the other children on the street, friends from school, and with our cousins, sometimes I enjoyed nothing better than being alone with a good book. I loved books about adventure and excitement, like Enid Blyton's *Famous Five* and *Secret Seven*, or funny ones like *The Diary of Adrian Mole*. I do not think I ever came across a single book with a character like me in it. There were no stories about mixed-race girls that I can remember, let alone girls with a disability like mine. I did not care, though. I loved imagining myself doing things that I would never achieve in real life, like abseiling down a cliff wall, caving or paragliding; doing whatever was necessary to find the clues that would lead to a dramatic ending in which a villain was uncovered, and I saved the day.

In recent years, Enid Blyton's books have been accused of being racist, and I think that they are less popular than they used to be, although that is probably largely because children have so many more reading choices nowadays. I am not sure that the accusation is fair – Enid Blyton's books were already quite old-fashioned when I was a little girl, and she was just writing from her cultural context of the 1930s to 1950s, when England (where she lived) was not as multicultural as it is now and few British people thought critically about the British Empire the way many do today. I would like to think that we could learn from the mistakes of the past without condemning everyone who lived in a different time, and nobody can take my fond memories of reading Enid Blyton away from me.

Because everyone knew that I loved reading, I was given lots of books for Christmas and birthdays, and we were also members of the local library, which seemed to have an inexhaustible supply. I also pored over popular girls' annuals like

Judy and *Bunty*, Irish ones like *Solas* and *Sugradh*, and even Dad's music magazines. I hugely enjoyed listening to music, although I think that my performance on the recorder at school confirmed that, like Dad, I was not born to be musically gifted.

On rainy days when playing in the street was not convenient, Ciara and I watched television. I loved anything with Shirley Temple in it, and we both adored *Button Moon* – an animated show on the BBC about characters who were also kitchen utensils – *Blue Peter* and *Take Hart*, which was a programme about how to make your own arts and crafts at home, featuring a cartoon man made of plasticine. Ciara and I were always sure that we were going to make all the things they demonstrated, and would busily assemble little collections of cardboard cylinders from inside toilet rolls and other supplies. Almost invariably, we lost interest before we ever made anything and the arts supplies would end up in a heap among the piles of gifts we had received at Christmas: my Fresh 'n Fancy make-up kit, boxes with snakes and ladders and tiddlywinks, and the Christmas annuals that we had already read a hundred times and were beginning to grow out of, but wanted to keep anyway.

When the Ethiopian famine struck in 1983, there was loads of television coverage about how many people were starving, and concerted efforts to raise money for the victims. It was strange for me to see people who had hair and skin like mine, but who lived far away, and in very different circumstances. As I always did when I saw Black people on television, I wondered if some of those on the screen might be related to me, and I hoped that they would be OK.

In 1984, the Irish pop star Bob Geldof was appalled by what he saw, and organized Band Aid to raise money for

Ethiopia. The following year, he put on the Live Aid concert with some of the biggest, most famous bands of the time, and secured himself a place in history as someone who did his best to help. On a swell of national pride and in absolute horror at what was happening in Ethiopia – and perhaps partly because of our folk memories of the famine that happened here in the 1840s – the Irish raised huge sums of money. There was so much press coverage at the time that everyone, even quite small children, knew what was happening and talked about it a lot. Inevitably, for some months after that, when most Irish people met a Black person, their minds naturally went to what they knew about the Ethiopian famine. It could be difficult at times, especially for someone little and thin like me, to be associated in people's heads with such an awful situation.

Foreign holidays, which had once been out of the reach of most ordinary Irish families, were now increasingly common, and I feel very lucky to have gone on plenty of them. While Irish people were travelling more than before, lots of my classmates had never been abroad, so we were fortunate indeed. Mam and Dad loved to travel, and both Ciara and I caught the bug from them. They brought us to Blackpool, Wales, and even to Spain, France and the United States. Before the trip, I would get so wound up that I would become anxious to the point of getting sick, and Mam and Dad learned that it was better not to tell me about it too far in advance.

I loved every minute of our trips: seeing new places, having new experiences. I can still remember the magic of the bright lights in Blackpool, the beautiful scenery in Wales, and how exciting it was to go to France and Spain and see people who looked different to Irish people, hearing them speak languages that I could not understand. In Spain we stayed in hotels or holiday villages with outdoor pools, and Ciara and I would want to linger in and around the water all day long, where we invariably made friends with all the other children on holiday, and had an absolutely brilliant time. Once, we had a connecting flight in London's Heathrow Airport. I will never forget walking through the concourse with my family, and looking with wonder at all the people of different ethnic backgrounds. I was used to being the only dark-skinned person I knew, and had never even been in a room with another Black person in it, but Heathrow was filled with people of every sort – tall people and short people of all skin colours and every imaginable combination of hair and eye colour, speaking all kinds of languages. For the first time in my life, I did not stand out in the crowd.

Seeing other places where people looked a bit different, ate different types of food and did different sorts of things, sometimes made me wonder about what my biological relatives' lives were like. From time to time I pondered why none of my mother's relatives in Dublin ever came to find me, to see what I looked like and check that I was having a good life without any of them. I decided that perhaps they had just forgotten I had ever existed, or wondered if they even knew about me. But I was especially curious about my relatives in Africa, about whom I knew absolutely nothing, and I thought about them much more often, and at greater length. I knew that I could assume that my biological mother's life was at least somewhat like Mam and Dad's, and that she lived in a house a bit like ours, but Africa seemed so mysterious and thrilling to me that it provided me with countless hours of speculation.

Whenever there was a documentary on television about

somewhere in Africa, my ears would prick up and I would sit down to watch it. If the film showed tribal people living in small villages of thatched huts, I would think that maybe that was how my relatives lived too. I would imagine how they would react if I suddenly appeared among them. Would they take me hunting? Play their drums and dance for me? Show me how to take care of their herds of goats, or offer me a glass of fresh goat's milk? Perhaps the people in the documentary were my *actual* relatives? Maybe, completely unawares, I was watching and listening right now to an uncle or an auntie who had no idea that I even existed. Or maybe they *did* know that I existed, and when they talked to the film crew, they had secretly hoped that their lost relative would watch them on the screen one day, and feel a sense of connection. I looked at the black or dark-brown skin of the people on TV and compared it to mine, feeling envious. I knew that my brown skin would never be as dark as theirs, and I thought that theirs was beautiful.

Other times, I would imagine that I was the daughter of a wealthy African prince, and think about the gorgeous palace he surely lived in, with sumptuous gardens filled with lush fruit trees and tinkling fountains. Perhaps, one day, I would get to visit, and my handsome father – beautifully dressed in a fancy suit or in ornate African robes – would explain why he had left me at the mother and baby home, to be fostered by the Penroses.

'I knew that you would be safe with them,' he would say. 'I'll never be able to express my gratitude to Noeline and Michael for taking care of my precious daughter. They are truly wonderful people.'

Then my father would ask me if I wanted to go and live in Africa with him and I would say nah, that I was grand where

I was, thanks, but Mam and Dad and Ciara and me might visit him the odd time.

But, mostly, I was perfectly happy to be Marguerite from North Dublin and did not give my biological relatives a second thought. While we were all open about the fact that I had not been born to the Penroses – not that we could have pretended otherwise – it seemed that all the books I read and TV shows I watched, and everything that we learned in school about what a family looked like, were just about a mam and dad and some kids, and of course that was exactly what I already had, even if I did not look like my sister or my parents. Most of the time, my biological relatives just seemed to belong to a different part of my life.

My memories of the last few years in primary school are a bit of a blur – a whirlwind of birthday parties, picnics, and bedtimes filled with giggles as Ciara and I were sent upstairs and kept one another awake for longer than we should have. In our second-last year of primary, we moved to Portmarnock, another North Dublin suburb, further from the city centre and closer to the sea. The new house was bigger than the old one, and while Ciara and I missed our friends from the street (although we continued to see several of them, particularly Yvonne, very often), we were also quite excited about our new home, which had shutters on the windows that I thought were very sophisticated, and a nice big garden.

Just days after moving in, Ciara and I were already good friends with Ashley from next door, who was exactly a year younger. Before long, we knew everybody, just like we had in Donaghmede. Although we were a little further away from our grandparents than before, we still saw them often, and sometimes Nana Josie would come to stay for a night or two.

Our old red setter, Mandy, had died of old age and we had a new dog, Lady. When Lady arrived as a puppy, she was so small that Ciara and I treated her like a baby or a fluffy, animated toy. We found an old woolly hat that nobody wanted any more, and used it as a sort of baby sling to carry our puppy around the house.

Life was just as sweet in the new house as it had been in the old one, and we also fitted quickly into our new school, St Helen's, which we joined in fifth class, just after Christmas. As before, Ciara and I were in different classes. I was surprised and delighted to find that, for the first time in my life, mine was not the only brown face in the room, as there was a girl called Catherine in my class whose dad was from India. Because we had a similar complexion, sometimes people asked me if I was Indian too.

The next school year, sixth class and our final year in primary, Ciara and I did our confirmation in Portmarnock with our new classmates. Mam bought us fashionable outfits in true eighties style: shoulder pads, drop-waist dresses with huge collars, hats and – to my absolute pride and delight – white lace fingerless gloves like Madonna's. Auntie Angela had come shopping with us to choose the outfits, saying that she loved to have a girly outing, because all of her children were boys who did not care less about clothes. (When Auntie Angela was pregnant with Darragh, her youngest, a couple of years later, we all pretended that we knew she was expecting a girl, and I used to call her bump 'Kimberley'. Still, we forgave Darragh for being a fourth boy – maybe partly because Auntie Angela had Ciara and me to go shopping with.)

On the day of the confirmation, Ciara and I posed proudly in our new outfits for a photograph, our first handbags dangling awkwardly from our arms. The top of my head, with my white hat perched on my black curls, came to just above Ciara's elbow, because I was still very petite, and Ciara had been through a growth spurt and was beginning to look like a young woman.

All my life, I had been much smaller than my sister, and now that we were approaching our teen years, Ciara shot up even more, while I stayed the same. I was always delighted when I grew into clothes that had become too small for her because that meant I had twice as many clothes – the new ones bought for me, and the ones that Ciara had only worn for a while because she was growing so fast. I always wanted to grow into her shoes too, but my gammy feet were a different shape to Ciara's and I was never able to wear them, much to my disappointment. But Mam would never have let me wear Ciara's old clothes for a special occasion, and always made sure that we both had lovely new things.

Mam and Dad had prepared Ciara and me for puberty and the various ways in which our bodies were going to change, and we were not particularly fazed when it all started to happen. I think I felt that, as my body had already been through so much, growth spurts and starting my periods were really no big deal in comparison. But, as I entered adolescence, I did develop a feeling of self-consciousness about my looks for the first time in my life. Visits to the seaside had always been a feature of my childhood, and now we lived on the coast and could go to the beach whenever we felt like it, but I never wanted to put on a swimsuit and reveal my scoliosis to the world. I did not resent my body for being different to the other girls', and I never let my petite size or curved bones stop me from doing whatever I wanted to, but at the same time, the thought of strangers seeing me in a swimsuit, realizing what had happened to me and feeling sorry for me – the thought of them not understanding that, in fact, I had a wonderful, enviable life – was more than I could bear. I told everyone, including myself, that I just did not like swimming or the seaside, but I think we all knew there was more to it than that.

Mam and Dad had always told me that when strangers stared at me, as they often did, it was because they thought I was a gorgeous little girl. I was beginning to realize that, while this might sometimes have been true, sometimes they stared for other, less kind, reasons too. I did not voice my feelings to Ciara, but I think she understood anyway. Having grown up together, sharing a bedroom for years, our bond was so close that we were often able to communicate without saying a word. A glance from one to another was enough. Ciara never nagged me to go swimming with her.

Ciara and I had a blissful summer after leaving primary school, and then it was time to move into secondary. Because we had only recently arrived in the area, Mam and Dad had not put our names down for the local school, which was minutes away and would have been extremely convenient, were it not for the fact that it was oversubscribed. Mam went and pleaded with the principal to let me in, at least, because I could not walk quickly, or very far, and a long journey on public transport would be very difficult for me. He said that his hands were tied, and that he would be in trouble if he let in a child who had just moved to the area ahead of one who had been on the waiting list for years, even if walking long distances was a struggle. So, Ciara and I were enrolled in Santa Sabina girls' school in Sutton, which was quite far away.

As summer drew to a close, Mam brought Ciara and me to a shop in Clontarf to get our new uniforms for Santa Sabina: a green jumper and skirt, a white shirt and a tie, as well as a smart blazer and a gaberdine. Of course, there was absolutely nothing in my size.

'I'm going to look terrible, Mam,' I said. 'All the other girls will laugh at me.'

I was looking at myself in the mirror at the shop. I had tried on the smallest green skirt they had, and it was so loose around the waist I had to hold it up, and so long that it was pooling on the floor around my feet.

'Oh, they all wear them big in first year,' the lady in the shop said encouragingly. 'She'll grow into it in no time.'

'I *won't*, Mam,' I said desperately. 'I'm never going to grow into this. Nobody will believe that I'm old enough to be in secondary school. I'll look younger than everyone else and they'll all laugh when I walk in.'

'Nonsense,' said Mam firmly. 'You'll look gorgeous. Don't worry, I'll get it sorted. We'll get it all adapted to your size.'

Mam bought me everything – skirt, jumper, blazer, gaberdine coat, the lot – and brought it to a seamstress who measured me carefully and remade the garments almost from scratch to fit my tiny, awkward frame. It cost Mam an absolute fortune, but true to her word, by the time the seamstress had finished her work, my uniform fitted me perfectly, and I looked absolutely fine and had just the confidence I needed to walk into school that first day alongside all the other girls.

Because of the distance, a school bus collected us at the seafront to bring us to school, and Mam or Dad generally drove us down to the bus stop. Once in a while I insisted on walking home from the bus, but I always regretted it, because it took me so long, and while Ciara was endlessly patient with my slowness and carried my school bag, as well as letting me lean on her for support, I felt bad about it.

Soon, Ciara and I had settled into school. I got along well with most of the teachers, and enjoyed English, and especially writing essays. I loved home economics, and was quite good at it because Mam had already taught us how to do so much. Although I do not think I was particularly talented at it, I liked art. We all loved Miss Cassidy, the art teacher, because she was so flamboyant with her bright blue eyeliner and henna-dyed red hair. Maths, on the other hand, did not agree with me. I absolutely hated it. Sports and PE, of course, were a no-go area. Much as I would have loved to run and jump with the other girls, I just was not able to. In primary school, I had always been encouraged to join in to the best of my ability, to do things slightly differently if I could not manage the same feats as my classmates, but now that we were teenagers, sports were getting more competitive and the students were expected to be athletic. I would never have been able to keep up.

I was still as sociable as I had been in primary, and I had loads of friends, not just in my own class, but throughout the school. Of course, just like the kids in our primary school, the girls at Santa Sabina were curious to know all about me because I looked different and was completely unlike my sister. As we were all older now, they knew about fostering and adoption and often realized that I had been born to other parents as soon as they saw Ciara. Mostly, they wanted to know where my biological parents had come from. They were less forward with their questions because, being older, they understood that not everyone wanted to talk about things like this. I did not really mind, though. I repeated the explanations that Mam and Dad had always given me, and that seemed to satisfy them.

Although I am sure that Mam and Dad have their stories to tell, I do not think that Ciara and I caused them much difficulty as teenagers. As far as I can remember, our close relationship with our parents continued undisturbed. From our point of view, it certainly helped that Mam and Dad were so indulgent in many ways, which meant that we had very little to feel grumpy about. They never said no when we proposed a sleepover, and there were often loads of girls spending the night on the floor of the bedroom that Ciara and I shared. While I consistently had lots of friends throughout the school, I also had my own little gang, and was especially close to a girl called Sandra. I also remained friendly with Catherine, the girl with an Indian father whom I had met in fifth class. I think that Catherine and I both appreciated one another partly because it was easier being one of the two dark-skinned girls in school than it would have been being the only one.

Sandra was a goth with blonde hair, pale make-up and dark eyeliner, and she was a quiet, thoughtful girl whose steady, gentle presence made me want to be her friend. We became very close the night we all got our Inter Cert results and went to Grafton Street in Dublin's city centre to celebrate. Sandra's family were warm and sociable, much like mine, and I became good friends with her older brothers Barry and Alan as well. We all started going to discos at the cricket club in Clontarf and to goth nights out. I loved the fact that she was such an individual. She knew her own mind and did not care what anyone thought – and she never cared that I was not a goth like her but just appreciated and accepted me for who I was.

Like all teenage girls, I started to become more image-conscious and wanted to wear fashionable clothes, just like my friends. This was the beginning of a struggle that has been part of my life ever since. Because of my size, most of the clothes that fitted me came from the children's section so, while my friends were starting to play with being glamorous and grown-up, I was still having to choose from a selection of little girls' clothes in bright colours with childish ribbons and bows. Because I did not want to show my scars, anything low-cut in the back was out of the question. So, although I loved fashion, I started to dread shopping for clothes. Mam helped me as much as she could by adapting the things that we got for me, but I always felt dowdy and plain compared to the other girls of my age.

Birthdays, as I said, had always been a huge deal in our family. The birthday girl always had a big party, and was not asked to do any household chores for a whole week. Even though my birthday was in January, just after the chaos of Christmas, I was used to being made a fuss of each time I got a year older. When I was small, I absolutely loved my birthday and felt very special, but now that I was in my teens, I started to feel a little differently about it. During the week or so beforehand, I would think about Elizabeth, the woman who had given birth to me, and wonder if she was thinking about me too. During that time, I would be quiet and, by my chatty standards, slightly subdued. The big day would come with all the usual celebrations and my mood would lift. When it was all over, I would be able to put aside the more difficult thoughts, at least for another year.

Mam and Dad had always encouraged Ciara and me to watch the news with them after the Angelus, as they felt that it was good for us to be informed about the world. I had never minded doing this, although for years most of it had gone over my head. Now that I was getting older, though, I was becoming more interested in current affairs, and more curious about what was going on beyond Dublin, Ireland, and everything that was familiar to me.

Understanding the wider world a little more helped me to see my own context more clearly. I had always felt different because of the colour of my skin, but the feeling had rarely bothered or annoyed me, and as a little girl I had known nothing about the history of race and racism. From watching TV, I knew that there were lots of Black people in America, for example, but I did not understand at first that this was because their ancestors had been taken from Africa and sold as slaves. I also knew that people in Africa were Black, and we were constantly reminded of the terrible poverty in much of the continent by the television and the various charities and missionary organizations that worked there.

As the 1980s progressed, we all knew a little about the apartheid government in South Africa because the riots there were often on the news, and workers at Dunnes Stores in Ireland had been on strike from 1984 to 1987 over the supermarket chain's importation of produce grown there. The strikes were often covered on RTÉ news and raised great awareness of apartheid among the people of Ireland. In our house, because of me, we were always drawn in particular towards stories that had anything to do with Africa. These early discussions about important issues of injustice, race and inequality had a big impact on me. I still did not understand what these big stories from history and current affairs had to do with me and my life as an Irish girl, but I was beginning to realize that, somehow, it was all connected.

7. Yeah, But Where Are You Really From?

As I grew into my mid and late teens, while I still lived in the comfortable embrace of my parents, my extended family and my school community, I became gradually aware of the fact that the images that most people saw of individuals who looked like me were negative ones, and that this was influencing how they saw me; influencing the sort of person they thought I was. Now I knew that some people did not like me, and never would, because of how I look.

During Lent and coming up to Christmas every year, Irish people were bombarded with advertising by charities and development agencies featuring images of photogenic black- and brown-skinned children dressed in rags, sometimes with dirty faces, with bellies swollen from malnutrition, or even with flies gathering in the corners of their mouths and eyes. These children stared at us, unsmilingly, from the photographs. The evidence of their own eyes told the Irish that Black people could never look after themselves, but always needed to be bailed out. At a time when Ireland seemed to be in permanent recession, a lot of people apparently found a sort of comfort in pitying others who were even worse off. Everyone, including me, appeared to think of Africa as a place of relentless pain and suffering and little else. This image was never balanced with stories of successful Africans – writers, artists, farmers, business people – who were living happy, fulfilled lives. A lot of people felt that, while slavery had obviously been bad, at least the American descendants of those slaves were now living in a wealthy country and did not have to deal with the perpetual challenges of the 'dark continent'.

When Irish people watched TV shows imported from America and Britain, they mostly saw actors who were as white as they were. Even when the shows had Black actors, they were often cast in stock roles that had very little nuance: the funny Black man, always making jokes and rolling his eyes comically; the angry Black woman, shouting and hilariously out of control; the frustrated Black youth, inevitably bound for prison and probably an early, messy death too. Black characters often featured as criminals, figures of fear, or as pitiful and poverty-stricken.

Of course, there were exceptions: Whitney Houston and Prince were huge stars at the time, for example, and *The Cosby Show* (Bill Cosby himself was not yet disgraced for his sex crimes, and the show was massively popular) depicted an attractive, middle-class, educated African American family in New York. However, the general impression most of the population had of Black people when I was growing up in Dublin was that they were typically either desperately in need or dangerous in some way, or perhaps both.

When it came to the representation of Black *Irish* people in the Irish media, there really was next to none, and it would have been easy for a little Black girl growing up in Ireland, with a less supportive family than mine, to feel different, to feel that she might never completely fit in at all.

Dad must have been very aware of how important it was for me to have role models who looked a bit like me. He loved Phil Lynott's music and we often played his vinyl records together in the sitting room at home. Phil was Black, and he was also undeniably Irish. Nobody but an Irishman would have produced that distinctive sound that was so of Dublin, and Phil, with his strong Crumlin accent, and the wicked twinkle in his eye, was very proud to be a Dub. At the same time, Phil's wild Afro curls, which were so like mine, his brown skin, and his facial features, which looked Irish and African at the same time, showed that, like me, part of him was from somewhere else; that his story was more complicated than most people's.

Dad and I were also fans of footballers Chris Hughton, who in 1979 had been the first mixed-race player to represent Ireland, and talented Paul McGrath, who had an Irish mother and African father, and had grown up in an orphanage before joining the Irish team and helping it to get into the World Cup. Kevin Sharkey was one of the few Black people on Irish television, working as a TV presenter on RTÉ. By highlighting the achievements of these men, Dad was pointing out the fact that one could be Black, Irish and celebrated, and telling me to be proud of being a Black Dubliner.

Because there were so few Black Irish people to whom I could relate, I also looked outside Ireland for role models and took an interest in the biographies of people like Nelson Mandela, Bishop Desmond Tutu, Angela Davis and Malcolm X, who had dedicated their lives to fighting injustice in their various ways. Perhaps partly because of having me, Mam and Dad were also very interested in politics and human rights, and we talked about those issues quite a lot at home. I remember the day – 11th February 1990 – when Mandela was finally released from prison after more than twenty-seven years behind bars. It was all happening very far away from Dublin, but there was a huge amount of media coverage and my whole family settled in front of the television to watch it, aware that this was a pivotal moment in human history. I can remember like yesterday that tall, slender man, unbent by all the years that he had spent in jail, smiling and waving as the South African national anthem played and the crowds cheered for him. Despite all that he had been through, it was clear that he was determined to look and move forward, and not to let the atrocities he had endured poison him.

I was also very interested in the careers of people like Spike Lee, Oprah Winfrey and Sidney Poitier, who had succeeded in the film and entertainment industry despite the prejudice against people who looked like us. I found the stories of my political heroes fascinating and inspiring, and was attracted by the experiences of successful African Americans who were at the peak of their careers despite the racism that was prevalent in the United States, but I could not always experience these as entirely applicable to me, as a young Irish girl growing up in Dublin, with Irish parents, an Irish accent and an Irish education. Aside from the colour of my skin – and the fact that sometimes people looked at me askance because of it – I had very little in common with African Americans. Yes, I had brown skin and Afro hair – but I did not grow up in an urban ghetto or in rural poverty in somewhere like Alabama, where most of the Black people are descended from slaves. While I was aware of racism and occasionally experienced it, I was never in danger of being followed home by the police, just because I was a Black girl living in a white neighbourhood. The problem was, there were very few public figures in Ireland who looked like me, and the world history curriculum that we studied in school barely mentioned Africa, other than some brief references to slavery in the United States.

Unconsciously, I started to scan the media for images that resonated with me. There were so few that I remember very clearly the ones that I found. Benetton, for example, was very fashionable at the time, and was one of the first big brands to feature models of all different physical types. Most fashion houses rarely used Black models, and when they did, they generally dressed them in leopard print or something else supposed to make them look 'exotic' or 'savage'. Or they made them pose with their teeth exposed in a snarl and their fingers curled up like talons, suggesting that they were a bit like animals, or somehow wilder and more dangerous than white women, who generally struck up more traditional sultry or girlish postures (a little later on, in the mid-1990s, the Spice Girls would appear on the scene and – surprise surprise – the one designated 'Scary', with animal-print clothing, was the only one with brown skin). It might seem like a small thing, but it meant a lot to me when Benetton advertised clothing with models from diverse backgrounds, including girls with Afro hair and brown skin like mine, and did not treat them any differently to the white models.

Simultaneously, I was becoming vaguely aware that sometimes white people could also be seen as 'other', if they did not fit the mould that everyone had decided was the right one. While there were no Traveller children at my school or in my area, sometimes Traveller women and children called to the door of our house, often on bitterly cold nights in the dead of winter, asking for help. Mam would give them toys and clothes that Ciara and I had grown out of and they would say thank you and go away. My parents never said anything negative about the Travellers, and I know that Mam had huge empathy for those women because they had such difficult lives, but I could tell that not everybody felt the same and that the friendliness and openness in Irish culture that people were so proud of, and that was so often praised as central to our way of being, did not extend to everyone. Similarly, young people from 'difficult' backgrounds were often rejected by most of society. When I was in my late teens, Mam and Dad briefly fostered a young man of fifteen. He had experienced a deeply traumatic childhood, not just because of his family's many dysfunctions, but also because society was not very accepting or understanding of the challenges facing people like him. He was a lovely boy who stayed with us for a year, and we were all very fond of him, and were sorry when he returned to his family, as he had been such a big part of ours.

While the message that I was getting from the world around me was that I might never be completely accepted as fully Irish, my parents were able to bring me the good news that – at long last – they were going to be allowed to adopt me and that I would become a Penrose in the eyes of the law. Due to my complex health issues and medical needs as a child, Mam and Dad had been advised not to start the process earlier, because as I was officially a ward of the state, the government was responsible for ensuring that I got all the healthcare that I needed. Now that I was sixteen, nearly seventeen, they were advised to adopt me quickly, before I turned eighteen and was legally an adult.

Mairéad, my social worker, came to our house to have a quick chat with me and with my family. I remember that day so vividly. Mam had already explained that there was going to be a lot of paperwork and that Mairéad would need to talk me through a number of things. Mam had warned me that nothing would happen overnight. Now she left Mairéad and me in the sitting room so that we could talk about what was going to happen.

Mairéad checked that I understood what was going on, and told me that my biological mother, after all these years, still had to sign an agreement stating that she was happy to waive all of her parental rights. All this time, I had been the Penroses' foster child, and my biological mother could have reclaimed me whenever she wanted.

'We don't expect there to be any difficulty,' Mairéad said reassuringly. 'But everything has to be done properly before the adoption order goes through.'

'OK,' I said.

I had not seen my biological mother since I was a tiny baby in the mother and baby home, and I had no conscious memory of her. It was quite scary to think that the final hurdle we had to clear before I could be adopted was her consent. What if at the last minute she changed her mind? She could still decide that she wanted to take care of me after all, and I could be summoned to another part of Dublin to live with a family I did not even know.

Thankfully, my biological mother did sign the form, and sometime after Mairéad's visit, we were given the all-clear. Via the social worker, my birth mother, Elizabeth, asked to see a photograph of me, and we gave her one. I wish now that I had asked for a photograph of her, although probably that would not have happened, as per her wish to remain anonymous. At the time, her signing the form seemed little more than a formality to me and I did not even think about it very much or imagine what she looked like. But I wonder what this moment was like for her. Was it hard? Did she cry? Or was she just happy to know that everything had worked out for me with the Penroses? I hope that knowing I was happy, and seeing my smiling face in the photograph we gave her, brought her some peace. My biological father was never mentioned. His name was not on my birth certificate, so in terms of the adoption, it was as though he had never existed at all.

Just a few days after my seventeenth birthday, my parents and I went to Apollo House in the city centre to finalize the paperwork. On the surface, I was quite blasé about the whole thing, so I acted bored and nonchalant. I had never felt anything but loved by my family, and I had always felt perfectly secure about being my parents' daughter, so it seemed completely normal and ordinary for them to adopt me. I dragged my feet as we went into the office, with its anonymous, dusty decor and the civil servant on the other side of the desk. I just wanted to get it over so that we could get on with the rest of our lives. The official explained what was going on to make sure that we all understood. We nodded and signed the papers and she gave us a copy of my adoption certificate, and that was that.

Deeper down, however, I think I realized what a big deal it really was. As I said, for years, I had always got a bit introspective around the time of my birthday. I would wonder about the woman who had given birth to me, and know that, wherever she was, she was wondering about me too. I think that I still had a lot of questions, but instinctively knew that I was not ready to hear them spoken aloud, let alone hear the answers.

A few days after the adoption, I was at my friend Yvonne's house in Donaghmede. So far as I knew, Yvonne and I had planned to go to a teenage disco with Ciara, but Mam rang and said that Ciara had changed her mind, and she invited Yvonne for a sleepover instead.

Back at our house, Mam was waiting for us.

'Go ahead into the sitting room, girls,' she said. 'I'll turn the telly on for you and you can watch it until Ciara comes downstairs.'

I walked into the dining room first and dumped my jacket on one of the chairs. I noticed that the chairs had all been moved against the walls and wondered vaguely why. Then I pushed open the door that gave on to the sitting room so that Yvonne and I could sit down and watch some TV.

'Surprise!'

My whole extended family, all of our close friends and many of the neighbours had gathered to throw a party for me, to celebrate the fact that, finally, the Irish state and legal system had recognized me for what I had been since I first came into their lives: Noeline and Michael's beloved daughter, and Ciara's sister. It turned out that my family had been planning the party for ages, and that Yvonne had been in on it too, keeping me out of the way so that they could get the house ready, and then bringing me back just in time for the big celebration.

My parents, my sister and all of our relatives and close friends looked at me with enormous smiles on their faces.

'Congratulations!' people said. 'What a wonderful day!'

Suddenly overwhelmed, I burst into tears and ran out of the room.

'Ah, love,' said Mam, following me. 'Everyone is here for you. We're celebrating your adoption! Today is your big day! Come on back and let's join in together.'

Everyone had brought cakes and sandwiches and delicious things to eat and I was the centre of attention all evening. My parents were beaming with pride and joy and I think, most of all, were just relieved that after all these years of loving me, they no longer had to deal with the nagging worry that somebody might try to take me away or tell them that I was not really their little girl. I never saw my social worker Mairéad again, and while she had only ever been kind, knowing that she would never again knock on our door and come in to ask questions about me and how I was doing made me feel very happy.

I finished school at the age of nineteen without a very clear idea of what I wanted to do. I had always enjoyed English and home economics, but when I tried to imagine a career for myself, I drew a blank. After the Leaving Cert results came out, we all went to the Debs. I brought my close friend Sandra's brother Barry, and she brought his best friend. I wore a milky-brown satin dress inspired by a famous TV advertisement for Galaxy chocolate that was airing at the time, with Nana Josie's pearl earrings and necklace. The party was held in the Shelbourne, followed by dancing in the Pink Elephant nightclub. We all felt very grown-up in our formal evening wear, although of course we look like children in the photographs.

The next autumn, still without a very clear vision for the future, I started a college course, studying social care and psychology in Senior College Ballyfermot. I had always been fascinated by how people's minds work and wanted to know more about that, and I had a vague idea that I might want to become a social worker after graduating. Mam and Dad felt that, if nothing else, the course would give me a good basic grounding that would be useful regardless of what I ultimately decided to do.

The college was on the other side of Dublin, and I had to take two buses to get there. Because this was really the first time I had started venturing around the city on my own, it was also the first time that I started using public transport without Mam or Dad. Most of my friends would hop on or off without giving it a second thought, but I was often a little anxious as I waited at the bus stop or sat on the bus. I had begun to notice that some of the other passengers did not want me there because of the colour of my skin, and I was also aware – though I did not want to admit it and hate typing the words even now – that I was physically frailer than others and would therefore be quite vulnerable if someone wanted to hurt me.

Sometimes it was the elderly lady who had been about to sit down beside me, but then took a look at my skin and hair and decided that she would rather sit somewhere else. Sometimes it was the old man sitting on the other side of the aisle who could not stop looking at me, and eventually got off, giving me a dirty sideways glance and muttering under his breath something I could not quite hear. Sometimes it was the woman who saw me and pulled her handbag a little closer, as though I might be going to grab it or take her purse out of it.

Once it was the man who spat at me because he did not like to see a Black person taking the bus or thought that my mere presence somehow sullied his experience of public transport. That was a particularly bad day. I can still remember the shocked look on other people's faces as what he had done registered with them. They glanced at each other, horrified. Then they gazed down at their feet, or out the window, or suddenly became very concerned with the contents of their bag or backpack. The last place any of them wanted to look was at me. Nobody said a word and, although I was completely surrounded by people, I felt utterly alone. I wiped the man's spit off, and made myself as small as possible until the bus reached my stop. I absolutely hated it when I felt that people were staring at me, whether because of the colour of my skin, because of my disability, or both. I just did not want the unwelcome attention at all, and it was that much worse when it came with a helping of racism. I am very petite, and very thin, and even people who are not that tall loom over me, which can make me feel extremely vulnerable. Sometimes, when people realized that I had caught them staring at me, they would feel embarrassed. They would look away or try to turn their attention on to something else. Sometimes men would act like they were looking at me out of concern because I did not seem happy.

'Cheer up, love, it might never happen,' they would say, or, 'Give us a smile,' or, 'You nearly gave me a fright, you look so bleedin' serious.'

I started to worry that maybe there was something wrong with the expressions on my face – despite being such a positive person overall, did I go about the place looking angry or pissed off?

One of the worst things about the unwanted attention was the way that other people reacted. If someone started saying things to me about my appearance, or behaving aggressively towards me because they did not like the way I looked, most people would respond by pretending that they were unaware of what was going on. Basically, the whole bus would pretend to be deaf until either I or the person who was hassling me reached our stop. I know that, like me, they were scared. They were afraid that if they spoke out, the situation might escalate and then they, as well as me, would be the target of the bully's aggression. Because I was scared too, up to a point I can see that this was understandable. But it would have meant an awful lot to me if people had found it in themselves to speak up.

Part of the problem, I think, was that racism was not really talked about much back then. We talked about it in my family because of me, but most people did not have a Black family member or close friend, and while they might have been familiar with the concept of racism, they did not see it as particularly relevant to them, or even to Ireland in general, and when they saw something racist happening right in front of them, they did not really have the vocabulary to understand it or to face up to it. As well as that, we have a long history in Ireland of pretending that everything is OK when it is not – of sweeping uncomfortable truths under the carpet and moving on. Of denying the role that we have collectively played in sustaining the injustices in our own society.

I caught the second bus to Ballyfermot outside the Virgin Megastore on Aston Quay, beside O'Connell Bridge. Usually, I bumped into a couple of my classmates at the stop, so at least I knew that I would be doing the latter part of the journey with company. Things were easier when I was with others because most racists do not have the courage to lash out against someone who is with a group of friends; they generally wait until you are on your own or with just one other person.

For most of my teens, I had been fairly quiet and happy to socialize with my family and with my friends from school and from our local neighbourhood. It was not really until I left school and started college that my social life took off. Now that I had college friends as well as school friends, I always had someone to go out with and I started to have a lively nightlife in the city centre. My best friend, Sandra, still lived in Clontarf, and I usually stayed with her when we were going out. We would get dressed up together, do our hair and make-up – it was always a struggle to find lipstick that suited me, because the fashionable colours then were pastels and ice-pinks, which looked ridiculous against my brown skin. Then we would meet up with our other friends, and take the bus in a group, hopping off in the city centre so that we could go for drinks in all the pubs that were popular with young people at the time, or go dancing at the Pod, which was a trendy nightclub. Life was quite exciting in those days, because we were all young together and the world seemed so full of possibility. In the middle of a sea of friendly people all the same age as me, I thought that it was easier not to be noticed – although because of my unusual appearance, the bouncers always recognized me, which meant that my friends and I were often bumped to the top of the queue. I was not as inconspicuous as I imagined or hoped. Despite my efforts to blend into the crowd, I never really did.

'Don't mind if people stare at you,' Mam often said. 'They're just curious. It's not really about you.'

But I did mind, although I pretended not to. I was getting sick and tired of always standing out, when all I had ever wanted was just to be accepted as the same as all the other girls.

Young girls out on the town, all dressed up and made-up, generally get lots of attention, and my friends and I were no exception. Most of the behaviour was normal flirting and chat, and we enjoyed it, but I had to deal with a whole set of questions and type of interest that my friends did not experience.

'Where are you from?' I was asked, again and again.

'I'm from Dublin,' I would say.

They would press me further for more information.

'I'm from Portmarnock,' I would say then. 'Northside.'

'Yeah,' they would say. 'But where are you *really* from? I mean, you're not Irish, are you? Not really. So, where are you from?'

A further complication was that the attention I got could be quite physically intrusive. I wore an Afro, and with my thick curls and dark skin, I was clearly mixed-race. People often wanted to touch my hair or rub it between their fingers. They seemed to forget that my hair was part of me, and that I might not always want it to be touched. It was fine when it was my friends – like all girls, we loved getting dressed up for the night out, and we swapped clothes and make-up and did each other's hair. But sometimes it was absolute strangers, coming up to me in the pub or in the nightclub or even on the street, and smearing their hands all over my head because they wanted to know what my hair felt like. I did not always know how to react. Often, I just froze and stood there while they patted me as though I was a dog, waiting for them to lose interest and go away, not wanting to make a scene and draw attention to myself because I absolutely hated it when everybody was looking at me.

Friday and Saturday nights in town are all about young people getting together, flirting, and sometimes pairing off. Of course, I often enjoyed it when I got positive attention from men of my own age who found me attractive. However, it was disturbing when they tried to use my Blackness as a way to chat me up.

'You're so *exotic*,' they would say, or, 'I love Black women, so much more attractive than white women,' or even, with a leer, 'Are Black women easy?'

Nothing was more off-putting than a man who expressed an interest in me just because I was Black, and did not care what I liked to talk about. I grew to hate the word 'exotic'.

Sure, it was used as a compliment, but it seemed to come with a load of baggage that I did not want to accept. I did not understand why those men even had to reference the fact that I am Black at all. Did they think I did not know already? Obviously, I am Black. If someone thought I looked attractive or that I was wearing a nice outfit, a compliment would have been lovely, but it did not have to come wrapped up in a discussion of my skin colour. Imagine how ridiculous it would be for a white woman to go to a club and get chatted up by some guy telling her that he loves 'white girls' for their 'unique look'. It is just as daft to say something similar to a Black woman – or man. I know that most of them were just curious and did not mean to offend me, but it got very tiring. Usually I would mumble an explanation and turn back to my friends. I have never understood why looking different seems to be interpreted by so many people as an invitation to make personal comments about someone's appearance.

One night, together with my friend Sandra and her brother Alan, I was on my way home from the Pod nightclub when a young woman emerged from a group to start screaming racist abuse at me, telling me that I was nothing, subhuman, and that I should fuck off home to where I came from. I knew that she did not mean Portmarnock.

I just stood there in shock and embarrassment while she yelled obscenities, wishing that I could disappear or rewind the evening and decide to go somewhere else instead. Her friends either stood there doing nothing or smirked. They were all very drunk. A crowd gathered around us all and, after a few minutes, another young woman stepped forward and confronted the screamer.

'Leave her alone,' she said. 'She's done nothing to you.'

I found my voice and told the uptight girl to go about her

business, that we were just going home after our night out, the same as her.

'I don't want any trouble,' I said. 'I just want to go home, OK?'

My friends joined in, saying that I had every right to be there. I could hear that they were getting angry, and became concerned that someone might attack Alan, the only man in our group.

'Don't get involved,' I whispered to him. 'Let me deal with it.'

I turned back to my abuser and tried to reason with her again. But instead of listening to me, she flew into a rage and attacked the young woman challenging her, punching her in the face.

Blood poured down my defender's face and she put her hands up to her nose as the attacker left the scene, dragged away by her friends, who had had enough. All of our attention turned to the poor woman who had confronted her, who was now completely covered in blood.

'Oh my God,' I said. 'I'm so sorry.'

I was absolutely mortified that this lovely girl had come to my defence and she had been attacked for it. I felt as though the whole situation was partly my fault. If I had not been there, being Black in a public place, none of this would ever have happened.

'Will you stop it,' she said. 'I didn't do anything apart from speaking up. She shouldn't have been talking to you that way.'

A couple of gardaí walked by and my friends and I told them what had happened. They asked us for a description of the girl who had been shouting racist abuse, and went off to see if they could find her, but I am sure that she was long gone by then, and there had been nothing distinctive or unusual about her. She was just one of thousands of young girls, dressed up for a night out with her mates. Racists look just like everybody else. The crowd began to scatter, and we went back to Sandra and Alan's house.

I was very upset about the incident – most of all, I felt awful that someone else had been hurt because of something that involved me – but I did my best to get over it, telling myself that it was an isolated event that did not mean very much, and that most people in Ireland were not racist and did not care what I looked like. The next morning, over breakfast, my friends and I discussed the horrible things that had occurred the night before and I told them that I was fine, that a random racist could not hurt me, although it had been upsetting at the time.

I *was* fine, in one way, but in another I very much was not. For months, whenever I went out, I was looking over my shoulder, wondering if someone was about to emerge from the crowd to have a go at me or tell me that I was in the wrong place. Even now, occasionally when I am out in town late at night, memories of that awful moment crowd into my mind and make me feel wary and ashamed.

While I loved the part-time work I did at a local Dunnes supermarket in Portmarnock, some of my experiences there also reminded me that I was seen as different. My colleagues at Dunnes were great – I was especially close to a lovely girl called Lydia, who is still a very good friend of mine – but once in a while a customer would see me behind the till, and then hastily take themselves and their trolley of groceries to another queue, apparently preferring to be served by a white girl, or maybe embarrassed by or feeling awkward about finding themselves so close to a Black person.

I know that very few of these people would have

considered themselves racists. Most of them were simply curious, because I looked different to the other girls, and they had only ever seen Black people on the Trócaire box or in other advertising for one charity or another. They had only ever encountered images of Black people in the context of material that presented them as utterly foreign and permanently in need of help. The idea of a Black Dublin girl, with a Dublin accent and an Irish family, was completely alien to them. It made no sense. For them, my appearance seemed entirely inconsistent with everything else about me. It simply never occurred to them that I might not want to be questioned about where I was from, that it was hurtful for me to see people notice my appearance and decide to move away, or that perhaps I was just as Irish as they were. That I could indeed be both Black and Irish. That there was nothing contradictory about it.

To some extent, I understood people's desire to know more about my story, and I often gave a brief explanation of how I had been adopted when I was asked to justify my presence. On the other hand, when I was on a night out with my friends, or just trying to get through my day, I did not want to have to explain, again and again, that yes, I *could* be Black and Irish at the same time. I often felt that I was being asked to excuse myself somehow, and that whether or not I was accepted was conditional on how I responded and on my showing a degree of deference, or even gratitude, just for being treated with a basic level of decency. In my own small way, I started to advocate for change, although my vocabulary for discussing the issues that I felt so strongly about was still quite limited.

I am a very positive person, and any of my friends will say that I am an optimist, confident, someone who loves company and always tries to see the bright side of things. All of that is true, but only up to a point. My outwardly confident behaviour springs from the coping mechanisms I developed in my late teens and early twenties, when I started to realize for the first time that a substantial number of Irish people would never completely accept me, just because of my appearance. Back then, I felt that I had only two choices: either I could slink away and become quiet and apologetic about myself, or I could smile and step forward as boldly as possible and show people that I deserve to be taken seriously, that I deserve to be respected. That Black people are not automatically aggressors, or pitiful, or to be feared and resented.

I had certainly absorbed the lesson that if I wanted to be accepted in certain circles, I would have to go above and beyond what was expected of someone who was white.

8. Adult Life in a Changing Ireland

Although I had enjoyed studying social care and psychology, when I graduated with a Higher National Diploma, I realized that I did not want to be a social worker after all. I knew that I would take my clients' problems on board, and that their problems would hurt me too, and then I would be no good to anyone. I had to come up with another plan.

I took a year off to think about what I wanted to do, during which I worked full-time in Dunnes Stores, stepping up from my part-time job while at college. Then, still not very sure about the direction I wanted to take, I did a year-long course on travel and tourism in Stillorgan College of Further Education on the southside. It dawned on me too late that I hated the course, but just as I was approaching the end, my friend Lorna told me that her employer, Ryanair, was looking for staff and there might be an opening.

'Do you think you might be interested?' she asked.

'Yeah,' I said, 'I'll give it a go.'

I interviewed for Ryanair, and was able to tell them that I already knew all about ticketing and other aspects of the travel industry, and I was hired.

Being a Ryanair employee, as you might imagine, can be a bit of a trial by fire. The staff are expected to put in very long hours, and to really give the job their all. The pay was OK, though considering how hard we all worked, it was not brilliant. But although it could be stressful at times, I liked the work, had a lot of fun, and found most aspects of it rewarding. In typical fashion for us, when a position was available, Ciara applied to Ryanair too, and soon we were working in the same business, just as we had studied in the same school for all of our childhood. We had lots of mutual friends and I think that people enjoyed how Ciara and I are so different, and yet so close at the same time.

Having started in ticketing, in the days when people still used physical, printed tickets, I moved through the company until I knew all the aspects of the business like the back of my hand. The only division I really hated working for was debt collecting for Ryanair Direct, because I found it very difficult being assertive and stern on the phone with people who owed Ryanair money. When I was moved to customer services in head office, right beside Dublin Airport, I knew that I had found my niche, as I was much more comfortable sorting out any issues people had. I did a six-month stint as a PA for the Director of Ground Operations because I wanted some experience in that area, but what I liked best was helping customers navigate their way towards a great holiday experience. I know that a lot of people complain about Ryanair, but the company has definitely made it much easier for ordinary working families to enjoy the sort of foreign holidays that wealthier people already know about, and because I love travel so much, I know how important that can be.

For me, working in Ryanair was an incredible learning experience, and there were a number of perks, including a certain amount of subsidized travel and six tickets every year that we were allowed to give to our friends and relatives so that they could take a break overseas. My colleagues were another huge perk. There were loads of fantastic people working for Ryanair, and I soon had many new friends. We

1. There are just three months between my sister Ciara and me. We've been inseparable since the day I became part of the Penrose family, aged three.

2. Mam and me, 1980.

3. Ciara and me in our matching shoes, 1980.

4. I was very fond of this stray dog, but we had to have him collected by the ISPCA a few days after this, 1983.

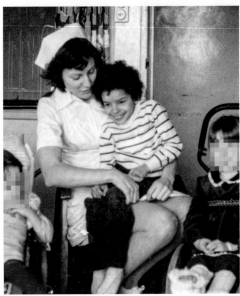

5. Ciara and me on our First Holy Communion day outside St Patrick's on the Navan Road, 1981. This is right outside the mother and baby home where I spent the first three years of my life.

6. Me, Nurse Aoibheann and two other patients in St Catherine's Ward at Crumlin Children's Hospital, 1982.

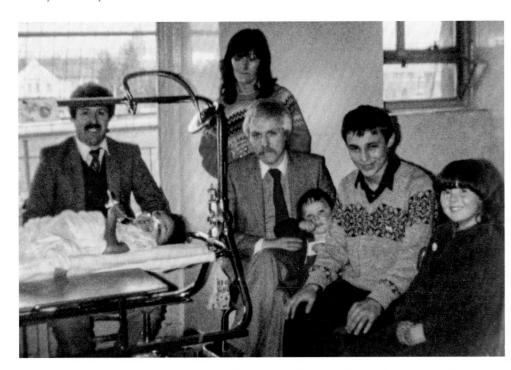

7. Me in hospital on a Stryker bed, which allowed me to be turned, 1981. I was glad to have a visit from Dad, Auntie Angela, Uncle David, my cousin Gary, Christian (a French student who was staying in our house) and Ciara.

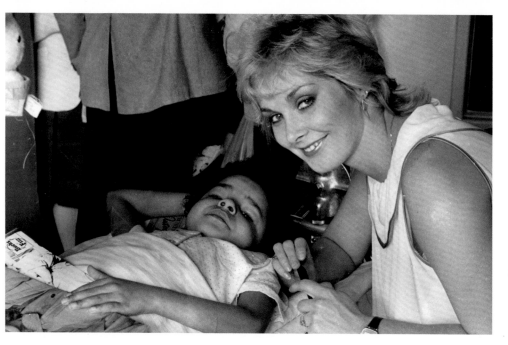

8. Making your mind up: after Bucks Fizz won the Eurovision in 1981, they came to visit us in Crumlin Children's Hospital. Here I am with Cheryl Baker. I was featured on RTÉ News with the band the day this photo was taken.

9. Nana Kitty took me to Lourdes when I was ten. The trip was incredible fun, though I didn't experience a miracle while I was there. It was my parents' persistence in helping me with my rehabilitation exercises that really allowed me to walk again.

10. Dad and me on a family holiday in Yugoslavia, as it was called back then.

11. Ciara and me enjoying the sunshine in County Clare, aged nine. Mam and Dad made sure the holiday was an exciting adventure for me, as it was for the rest of the children. No big mystery was made of the wheelchair, which was soon integrated into our games!

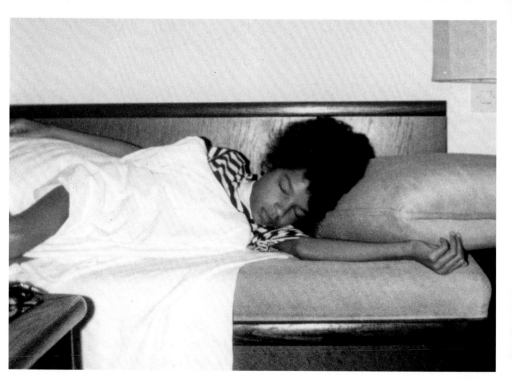

12. All tuckered out on holiday in Tenerife with the family, 1986.

13. Mam and I met these Laurel and Hardy lookalikes when we went to California in 1990.

14. Nana Josie, Ciara and me in Auntie Angela's house on our confirmation day, 1987.

15. Dad and me hanging out at Auntie Angela and Uncle Dave's house, 1992.

17. Ciara and me about to head out to our Debs, October 1993.

16. By sixth year I was rocking a pair of Doc Martens with my school uniform, 1993.

18. A family gathering at Auntie Angela's with all the cousins, uncles, aunts and great-aunts. The kids at the front are Gary, Sarah, Aisling, Rebecca and Conor.

19. Ciara's twenty-first birthday party – she's in brown – with our friends, sisters Yvonne and Lisa, who we've known since we were three! 1995.

20. Ciara and me about to head out on the town, around 1998. We were both working for Ryanair at the time.

21. My friends Alan and Sandra, who I've known since secondary school, 1999.

22. Mam, Dad, Ciara and me having a laugh in our house at Portmarnock, around 1992.

23. Mam, Dad and me at the wedding of my friends Yvonne and Dave, 2005.

24. In RTÉ Radio One with Ryan Tubridy when he interviewed me in July 2020.

worked hard as a team, but we never got sick of each other's company, and often met up at weekends and even went on holiday together. Sinéad, Rhona, Dickie, Paula, Erin, Michelle and Nicola are all still great pals of mine to this day.

I mostly used my subsidized travel to go to London, as I had friends there – Alan, John, Diego, Mairéad and Ed – and I have loved the melting pot that is London ever since my first encounter with Heathrow Airport as a young girl, when for the first time in my life, I did not feel like I was standing out, as I often did at home in Dublin. There were so few Black people in Dublin at the time that if I was out and about and saw someone else who looked a bit like me, I always noticed them, and often our eyes would meet. As I got to know London better, I grew to appreciate it on all sorts of levels: the fact that there were people there from all over the world, its huge diversity, and the way there is so much energy on the streets. I also loved the fact that I could get lost in the crowd, because there are so many different people, with such a wide array of physical types, that most of the time people do not even notice what you look like. Despite that, I was never tempted to leave Dublin for ever and make London my home. Much as I enjoyed my trips to London and the great times that I had with friends who lived there, I was also glad to get back to Ireland, and I am very proud of my native city and love the feeling of belonging to it.

Now that I had a permanent job, a decent salary and a rake of new friends – as well as all the old ones – my social life was even fuller than before. Dublin was like a playground for me then, full of great places to go. The Pod nightclub, with its sister venue, the Chocolate Bar, was still my favourite, and my friends and I went there often to dance to the music and socialize, but I liked all the others too. We typically started the evening in a pub, or with drinks in a friend's house, before we hit the dance floor.

Because of my physical limitations, going around town, and up and down the stairs to the various venues that we visited, could be more challenging for me than for others, but I always managed. To my mortification, though, when I went out with my friends, I still often encountered people who wanted to talk to me about why I have difficulty walking.

'Ah here, what happened to your back?' they'd say, or, 'Are you after breaking your leg?' or, 'You need to eat something, girl, there's not a pick on you,' or even, 'Were you in an accident? Show me your scars!'

I would do my best to be polite, although my disability and my scars were the last thing I wanted to talk about on my Saturday night out. Generally I would smile and try to change the topic of conversation. Sometimes they would get the hint and wander off or choose something else to talk about. But sometimes, if I did not answer them the way they wanted or expected, they would get annoyed and even become verbally aggressive.

'I'm only asking,' they would say. 'There's no need to be so sensitive,' or, 'Who the fuck do you think you are? I'm only taking an interest.'

While the constant attention and curiosity about my disability was always unwelcome and often stressful, I had learned how to deal with these comments by brushing them off and getting on with my life. I knew by now, from a lifetime of experience, that if I took my time and did things my own way, I could do anything. I just wished that other people could see that too.

Around that time – in the mid-1990s – I was inspired by a new hero when Christine Buckley emerged as one of the most powerful voices for Black and mixed-race Irish people that I'd ever heard. Christine was a generation older than me, and her childhood in an institution, Goldenbridge Industrial School in Dublin, had been marred by violence and abuse. As a child, she never had the happy family life that I did. To me she was (and has remained) a hero for overcoming her difficult past, for giving a voice to the survivors of Irish institutions in the film about her life, *Dear Daughter*, and for being a positive role model as a mixed-race Irish woman who was embracing her complex heritage and becoming a fearless advocate and activist. Because I spent the earliest years of my life in institutional care, I identified with her and admired her for her courage and dedication.

Ireland was changing very quickly in those days. In the 1980s, when I was a child, people had often said that Ireland was the poor man of Europe, and when the film *The Commitments* came out in 1991, one of the characters, Jimmy Rabbitte, said that the Irish were 'the Blacks of Europe', by which he meant poor, marginalized and seen as lower-class. Unemployment levels were very high then and a lot of young people just wanted to get out of the country and find good jobs overseas. But by the mid to late nineties, Ireland was getting much wealthier and much more closely linked to the rest of the European Union, and was consequently a more attractive destination for people looking for work and the opportunity to get on in life. For the first time that I could remember, there were quite a few Black people in the city centre, many of them migrants from African countries, as well as growing numbers of Asians of all sorts, and loads of migrants from other European countries, like Poland and

Estonia. Now I could go into town and see other people who looked like me and other women with hair like mine.

It was around this time that I had my hair chemically relaxed, having had Afro curls all my life so far. I loved my Afro hair in some ways but at the same time I had always wanted long hair. Most of my female friends had hair that they could wear up or down, tuck behind their ears, or hold back in a ponytail or a bun. With my dense curls, I thought I had fewer hairstyles to choose from.

By this point there were hairdressers in Ireland dealing with the needs and wants of the Black community, so there were some who had the skills to provide hair-relaxing treatments, although not as many as there are now. RTÉ had a TV show called *Head to Toe* that featured makeovers, and showcased the work of people like stylists, beauticians and hairdressers. One day, they did a makeover on a woman with an Afro like mine, turning her tight curls into a flowing mane of sleek black locks. I was so excited by her transformation that I wrote down the name of the hairdresser, Therese Coker, and booked an appointment with her. I went in to Therese with the Afro curls that had adorned my head since the day I was born, and came out with long, straight, black hair.

'Hello, Pocahontas!' Dad said when I got home.

My parents could not stop looking at me all evening. They had never expected to see me without my curls, and I looked very different now. I had always wanted long hair like Ciara's when we were young, and finally I had smooth, long locks that hung over my shoulders, as hers had done. It was nice, with my new hairstyle, to be able to go out to a nightclub or bar without people wanting to rub their hands all over my head to marvel at the texture of my hair. I enjoyed trying different styles and wearing it in a ponytail for the first time in my life. I have been going to the same hairdresser ever since, and our running joke is that Therese must never retire, because then I will have nobody to do my hair for me.

In the United States and much of the world, natural Afro hair is not seen as desirable. White teachers and employers often penalize students and employees for having big Afros, or for wearing their curly hair in traditional African styles, such as cornrows, and there is a widespread view that the natural hair of people of African descent just does not look 'professional'. The fashion for chemically straightened hair ultimately springs from a reaction to this situation. Today, it is the norm not just among African American women, but increasingly in Africa too. By getting my hair straightened, I was both identifying with the other Black women I saw, and participating in the collective ritual of taming our hair to make it more acceptable to the white majority.

At first, when I saw that there were more and more people from different backgrounds coming to Dublin to live, to work and to raise their families, I was delighted. Finally, I thought, Ireland was becoming more multicultural and diverse. It was refreshing not to have to endlessly answer questions about where I was from – where I was *really* from – as though I had ever been anything but Irish. But as Dublin's demographics changed, so did the reactions of a not insignificant number of people to the newer arrivals.

Now, lots of people, like me, absolutely loved what was happening in Ireland. All of a sudden, there were new hairdressers, looking after women with hair like mine, and catering to Irish mothers who had had children with African fathers and needed help learning how to do their daughters' Afro hair. Mam would have benefited from that when I was little because, while she did her best, there was nobody in those days to show her how to manage my wild curls, and I always wore them short so that they would not get too tangled. There were also loads of new restaurants, selling tastes, smells and experiences that seemed enticing to many of those who had grown up on bacon and cabbage and Irish stew. There were little grocery shops selling things like yams, mangos, coriander and lemongrass, serving the new communities but also delighting anyone who liked to cook and loved to try new flavours. Since childhood, I had been very curious about what the lives of my African relatives might be like. The new African-run grocery shops at least gave me a hint of what their favourite foods might be.

Swathes of the inner city that had become almost derelict since the huge exodus earlier in the twentieth century, when Dublin people fled tenements and flats for bigger, more comfortable homes in the suburbs, were now being rejuvenated by newcomers moving in from elsewhere, attracted by the lower rents to set up businesses and get a head start. Shops that had lain empty for years were being opened up and transformed, and streets that had been desolate were filling up with life. Walking down O'Connell Street, more and more I could hear all sorts of languages being spoken around me. It was very exciting.

But in parallel with these changes, a sinister undercurrent of fear, anxiety and anger was steadily growing. Some people looked at the rejuvenating inner-city areas, with their shops and restaurants selling things that had never been seen in Dublin before, and instead of thinking that it was great, and maybe that they would like to go into one and try something new, they said that these people – these foreigners, these outsiders, these unknowables – were coming over here and taking jobs away from decent, hard-working Irish people. And who did they think they were, with their ingredients and dishes that looked and smelled so different to what we were used to here in Dublin?

Some of them looked at the babies born to Irish women who had met African men, or African women who had met Irish men, and instead of cooing over their adorable chubby hands or their big brown eyes, or the fascinating way the features of their tiny faces were both Irish and African at the same time, they muttered about how these babies were not real Irish people; or about how people should stick with, and marry, their own because the children of mixed relationships would never know where they belonged; or about how African blood was diluting, or even polluting, the Irish race.

Some of them felt that it was not right for children of colour, or for children whose first language was not English, to attend local schools – and God forbid that those children might ever be in a majority in a particular class.

Some of them, as the 1990s turned into the early 2000s, pointed to the horrors of 9/11 in New York and suggested that something of the sort might happen in Ireland, now that we had so many people moving here from overseas, or hinted that people of colour were somehow naturally more inclined towards criminality and that, as our population became more diverse, it was inevitable that it would also become more crime-ridden. They suggested that we could keep crime down in Ireland by keeping those people out.

While I had been aware since my early childhood that I looked different and that people noticed me, now I was more on guard than ever, as I knew that negative reactions to people with brown and black skin were increasingly escalating to verbal abuse and even physical violence. It was not that these things happened often, because they did not – it was just the knowledge that the possibility was always there. That today might be the day when someone decided to lash out, and that I would be the one there to bear the brunt of their anger.

The vague ideas that I had held about race, racism and justice began to crystallize into something clearer. Much of what I had learned about these issues in Ireland had come from listening to and reading about Christine Buckley when I was younger. Whenever she was quoted in the newspaper, or whenever she wrote anything or spoke on the television, I listened carefully, because I knew very well that my generation was following in her footsteps, and that we owed her a lot. At the same time, with Ireland changing so much, and so quickly, we were also beginning to face new, different challenges of our own. It seemed to be easier for people to listen to Christine Buckley and empathize with all that she had been through than to see other people, with less familiar accents and cultures than their own, and to understand that their stories mattered too; that their experience was also, increasingly, an aspect of what modern Ireland is all about.

I was fiercely independent, but I was still living with my parents at this stage in my life, my early and mid-twenties. I loved travelling and had started venturing off and having adventures of my own – a trip to America, another to Australia, frequent trips to London. A lot of people I knew, including my cousin Alan, had gone to America for a few months. Alan was staying in San Francisco with a group of friends, and I had a great time visiting them and seeing the city. Of all the places I went to then, I think I loved New York and Australia the most.

It was always a huge pleasure to see my friends, and to

explore their new lives together with them – but I also loved coming home, and no matter how much fun I had had on my holiday, I unfailingly experienced a thrill when the plane started to descend over Dublin and the familiar contours and shapes of my hometown began to reveal themselves through the clouds.

I never had any difficulties travelling around the world but getting around Dublin on public transport could be an ordeal. Mam insisted that I should be able to travel easily by myself, pointing out that it was an issue of quality of life. She put her foot down now and insisted that I learn to drive so that I would not have to rely on anyone or anything to get to where I needed to go. She pointed out that being a good driver was more important to me than most people, because I find walking and using public transport so tiring. After a long and exhausting day at Ryanair, the last thing I needed was to have to stand at a cold bus stop, waiting for the bus to come.

'Put your coat on,' Mam said one winter night. 'We're going out.'

'Where are we going?' I asked.

'You're having your first driving lesson.'

It was dark, miserable and rainy out, and I was absolutely terrified. But two weeks later, I realized that Mam was right, and that driving was going to be a fantastically liberating experience for me. I have been a happy driver ever since, and now I cannot imagine life without my car, which makes it possible for me to get to work quickly and easily and to visit my friends whenever I want.

Then Mam and Dad decided to leave Portmarnock, where Ciara and I had spent our teen years, and buy a new house in Bettystown, Co. Meath. They liked the idea of being near the city, but somewhere a lot greener and more rural. Dad loves gardening and he would have more space to garden in, and they both looked forward to having lots of countryside to go for long walks. I grumbled a bit about the new location, which seemed like the back of beyond to me at first, but as I was still living at home then, I made the move with Mam and Dad. I could see why they loved Bettystown, which is near the sea and surrounded by beautiful scenery, but after a little while I felt that, as I was getting older, I wanted to live independently from my parents. I moved back to Dublin, where I rented a room from a friend, Rachel, and set about enjoying life.

As I broadened my physical horizons, I was also increasingly curious about the world around me, and about different ways of doing things. I was fascinated by alternative therapies, and in particular the spiritual aspect of health and self-knowledge. I had always been drawn to meditation and psychology, using positive affirmations to inspire myself and maintain a happy outlook on life, and in general to those aspects of life that can be tricky to understand and quantify. I already knew how powerful it can be to use affirmations, and often turned to them when I was having a tough day at work. Just saying to myself something like, 'Today is a good day, you are a good person, and you are doing your best,' or, 'This is not a bad day, it is a bad couple of minutes,' or, 'I have the strength to get through whatever comes at me today,' could reset my mood if I found myself beginning to feel down. Nobody's life is perfect and easy a hundred per cent of the time, and we all have to find a way to cope with the challenges that are presented to us.

I also started to study with a reiki master called Berni Dolan. Berni attuned me to reiki and also introduced me to more advanced meditation and taught me the many health and emotional benefits from practising it regularly. Working with Berni, and meditating with her meditation group, was a total break from the stress and frantic pace of Ryanair, and I continued moving through reiki Levels 1and 2 with her. I still occasionally do reiki for friends, and meditation has been part of my daily routine ever since.

Around this time, I also visited a medium who did a reading for me. While I was in his room, I started to feel strange. The man smiled at me and said not to worry, that there was a huge angel in the room, watching over me. Well, I was completely overwhelmed by the powerful presence and by my body's reaction to it, although the medium assured me that I had no reason to be afraid. I did not know what to make of that. Was it a sign of the fact that, in so many ways, I have had a blessed life?

As I moved into and out of my late twenties, my friends and I went through one milestone after another. At one point, so many of my friends were getting married that I went to sixteen weddings in two years. A lot of the ceremonies were held overseas, and I visited Italy, Croatia, Mauritius and some other wonderful destinations to attend them. Ciara married her fiancé, Dave – of course, our party-loving family celebrated the occasion, a traditional Irish wedding, with aplomb – and they were looking forward to starting a family.

While shopping for dresses to wear to all these weddings in styles and shapes that would suit me was always a challenge, I absolutely loved the ceremonies and the parties afterwards, and then, of course, the babies who often followed a year or two after the honeymoon. I was always delighted to meet the newborns and to examine their little faces for resemblances to their parents.

Ciara got pregnant about four years after her marriage. It was so exciting knowing that I was going be an aunt. Jamie was a gorgeous, chubby child who looked just like his mam, and Ciara was brilliant with him from the start. She had always wanted to be a mother, and she was an outstanding one. Ciara asked me to be Jamie's godmother, and I was so happy when I stood for him on the day of his baptism. A few years later, Charlie was born, and Ciara's little family was complete. My two nephews have been making me proud ever since. I love talking to them, playing with them, and seeing how much they resemble my beloved sister and brother-in-law. It is an honour to be in their lives as they grow up and become men.

Yet, while I was happy for Ciara and my friends, and while they sometimes joked that they knew I would settle down when I finally found the right person and that my standards were just too high, I never envied anyone else's life.

People with disabilities all have extra hurdles to deal with when it comes to our love lives. We can feel self-conscious about the way we look, and worry that we will not come across as attractive to others. But while men with disabilities certainly have their own anxieties and concerns, for women with disabilities there is a whole other layer of complication, because we also have to consider whether we can be or want to be mothers, whether it would be safe for us to experience pregnancy, and whether we are willing to take what are often considerable risks.

I had never actually been told as a teenager or young woman that pregnancy was not an option for me, but at the same time I was not stupid, and I knew that it would be very dangerous for someone with my condition. I never made a conscious decision not to become a mother, but on some level I always knew that it would not be a good idea for me. While I have a full and fulfilling life, I have always lived with challenges that include the fact that my lungs are compressed inside a too-small torso, which can make breathing difficult; that several of my ribs are made of titanium; and that my curved spine and limp put huge pressure on my frame, every single day. Somewhere in my gut, I just knew that my body was not made to carry a child. I knew that, were I to become pregnant, the outcome for my health would be extremely uncertain, to put it mildly. I would probably have to spend most of the pregnancy in hospital, and I absolutely hate being in hospital. And, even if I did manage to carry a child safely to term, there was no guarantee that pregnancy and childbirth would not damage me to the extent that I would struggle to care for a baby. From early on, I had no doubt that these were risks that I was not prepared to take and I accepted this from the outset.

Another issue that I still lived with was self-consciousness about the shape of my body and the many scars on my back, my sides, the sides of my head and on my knees. This had been very difficult for me in my early and mid-teens, when I had just wanted my body to be 'normal' and ordinary and had found it hard to buy fashionable clothes that suited my body shape and did not make me look like a little child. I know that everyone can be self-conscious about their looks at times, but when your body is as different as mine is, accepting it uncritically can be challenging. I had become a lot better about shopping for clothes over the years, and less anxious about my looks, but if I am being brutally honest with myself, my self-consciousness probably did play a role in the fact that I tended to maintain a certain amount of distance from the men I met. If someone started chatting me up when I was sitting in a bar, I would immediately start to worry about what would happen when I stood up to get a drink, and he realized that I have scoliosis. Partly because of these feelings, I tended to shy away from relationships. On top of all that, my number-one coping mechanism as someone who has never wanted to be underestimated, and who knows that she is much tougher than she looks, has always been to show a fierce independence. Mam used to tease me about how fussy I was.

'You're waiting for a prince to ride up on his horse to you!' she used to say.

I would just laugh, because – although I definitely am romantic – I was happy to wait until the right person came along, and happy if he never did. Everyone in my life knows that if I want something done, I will do it myself. I might not always be able to do it in exactly the same way as other people, but I will get there in the end. I do not like to ask for help and I do not like to feel dependent on others. I hate it when people think that I cannot do things on my own, and most of the time I manage to prove them wrong. So, as I moved through adulthood, I did so as a happy, confident, fulfilled woman who knows that she has made the right decisions. I respect mothers hugely for all that they do, while being quite grateful that I have never had to do any of it myself. While I have many male friends, and huge love and respect for them all, I have never felt that I needed a husband or a long-term partner to be complete.

Still, with each little baby that came into my life, whether they were a new relative or the child of a beloved friend, I always thought about my biological mother, about Elizabeth, and how difficult it must have been for her to give birth to me, only to hand me over to an institution even as her breasts filled with milk intended for me, and while she was still bleeding and sore from having given birth. There is something so beautiful about how a new mother bends her head over her tiny child, about the way that tiny child gazes up at her. I suppose that my biological mother and I might have shared a few of those moments in the hospital at the very beginning of my life, before I was taken out of her arms for the last time and brought to the nursery in the mother and baby home. Before I was sent to the 'reject room' where the children who couldn't be adopted were kept.

By the time I reached the age of thirty, almost all of my friends had moved into their own places, and I was still living in a shared rented house in Dublin. One weekend I came home to Bettystown, and Dad said that Mam wanted me to go and look at some apartments that were being built around the corner.

'Why?' I said. 'I live in Dublin – I'm not moving back to the countryside!'

But when Mam got back she insisted that the new apartments were lovely, and that Bettystown was a fantastic place to live, and the next day I found myself viewing a show apartment together with Mam, Ciara and Dave.

'Isn't it gorgeous?' Mam said. 'Your dad and I think that it's time you got on the property ladder.'

I had had no intention of buying anywhere, but when I thought about it, I could see that it made sense. Mam and Dad were so happy in Bettystown that Ciara and Dave, and then my Auntie Angela and Uncle David, had all decided to move there too. Sure, I had a great social life in Dublin and most of my friends lived there, but Bettystown was just up the road from the city, property was way more affordable, and I knew that I could spend the night at a friend's house anytime I wanted. What could be better, I realized, than living surrounded by the people who love you most?

The very next day, Mam and Ciara put down a deposit for me and, just like that, I had my own home, a lovely ground-floor apartment that opened straight into the complex's garden area. Having to pay the hefty mortgage every month was a bit of a wake-up call, but Mam had been right. It was great to have a place of my own.

9. Jack of All Trades

After being with Ryanair for eleven years, I was exhausted. In 2008, I went to Thailand on a two-week holiday with my friend Lydia. I had known Lydia for a long time, since we met working in Dunnes. For years she had been telling me that I needed to change jobs, and she took the opportunity to tell me again.

'All you ever do is work,' she said. 'You need a less stressful job.'

Hearing her words while I was on holiday, feeling stress-free after a few days off, I could see that she was right. Ryanair had been good to me in many ways, and I will always be glad about the time I spent there, and grateful for all I learned on the job, but there is more to life than work, and I was ready to move on.

After we came back, I finished up at Ryanair and found a job in a bridal shop in Baldoyle, North Dublin, selling wedding dresses, veils and all the rest of it, as well as a range of formal wear for men and for special events like confirmations and Communions. My boss was a designer, and many of the dresses were her own creation. Initially, I was hired to work as the office manager, but as time passed, I found myself increasingly on the shop floor. As someone who was happily single, now I was going to be helping brides-to-be to pick out the dresses that they would wear on what was supposed to be the happiest day of their lives. For most women, choosing their wedding dress is no trivial matter. After all, not only do they want to look gorgeous on the day, but they are going to be looking at that dress in their wedding photos for years to come.

I love chatting to people and, as I am my mother's daughter, I also love helping to organize a big party, so I really enjoyed the work at the bridal store and picked up a completely different skill set. As I got to know my boss better, I also accompanied her on buying trips and became quite expert in everything to do with wedding dresses. Overall, with the exception of our colleague Paddy, who did deliveries, it was a very feminine environment to work in and, while I enjoy male company, I loved the female energy and working with other women.

One of the more rewarding aspects of my job at the bridal shop was meeting the many Traveller women who came to the store to choose their finery. The Traveller community generally loves big weddings and all the girls wanted to wear something very glamorous. They always needed dresses with big skirts so that they could fit several hoops underneath to give them the profile they were looking for, frequently asked for extra Swarovski diamonds for that additional bit of bling and sought advice on tiaras and accessories. Often, they told me that they had come to us after having been treated quite badly in a number of other shops by assistants who made them so uncomfortable that they felt they had no choice but to leave. I never really understood what the problem was, because they were great characters and fantastic customers. Once the women had chosen their dresses, the father or uncle of the bride would come in to pay for them, as was their wedding tradition. This always involved a little haggling, but that was part of the banter. The thing I liked best about working with the Travellers was the fact that the whole family got involved in the wedding – aunties and uncles, cousins, the lot.

It reminded me of how I had been brought up, in the heart of an extended family that had always been there for me.

When we looked after brides who needed dresses in larger sizes, I realized that it is not only those with disabilities who can struggle to find options. I often met women who had been told by other shops that they should go away and come back when they had lost weight, because there was nothing for them in their size. I am glad to say that we always treated all of our customers with respect, and never tried to shame anyone into losing weight. Everyone deserves to look fantastic on their wedding day.

After five and a half years of working in bridal wear, I needed to have ligament surgery on my right ankle, because the way I walk, as a result of my scoliosis, puts huge pressure on my joints. Little by little, I was losing the ability to use my right ankle, and I knew that if I did not get treatment, eventually I would not be able to walk at all. I was still working full-time, but I was increasingly aware that soon I might not be able to do that either. I could not bear the thought of spending the rest of my life at home, restricted in my movements, so I told my doctors that surgery was no problem. All I wanted was to remain as mobile as possible. While I was not looking forward to being in hospital and having to endure the physiotherapy that I have hated since I was a child, I knew that having surgery was my only option.

Things had slowed down in the bridal-wear business as a result of the economic downturn, and I was made redundant shortly before Christmas 2013. While this was a bit of a blow, it was also a blessing in disguise, because I was scheduled to have the surgery in January and would need to take some time to recover.

The doctors warned me that, even if the surgery was a

success, this was a problem that was likely to recur, and that as my body got older, I would start to have more and more problems of this nature. They even explored whether another spinal surgery was still an option for me, now that I was in my late thirties, but to my relief the consultant who saw me said no, that I was too high-risk because of what had happened when I was in Crumlin Children's Hospital. As we left his office, Mam asked me if I wanted to see some other doctors, and get a second and third opinion. I knew that this would be a waste of time and that we both had to accept that my back was not going to change. Having surgery on my ankle so that I could walk more easily again was all that I could do.

The surgery was stressful, of course, as it always is, but as it had been quite difficult finding someone prepared to operate on me at all, I was just relieved that it was going ahead and hopeful that I would see a big difference. It was, however, a difficult and painful process. On the first attempt to carry out the operation, I had a bad reaction to the anaesthetic and had to spend a night being monitored in ICU. I lay there all night in a state of terrible confusion, my mind racing all over the place as a result of the drugs in my system and of my rapid heart rate and high blood pressure. As the bad reaction had come after surgery started, I also had an open wound on my ankle, barely contained by the bandages around it.

Opposite me in ICU, a middle-aged couple sat on either side of a bed occupied by a young girl who was lying completely still on the flat of her back with wires and tubes connected to every part of her body. She had taken an overdose earlier that day. Her parents wept and clutched at the soft blankets covering their daughter's body as the nurses and doctors provided them with updates about what they were doing and what the girl's prognosis was. As the drugs gradually left my system and I became more lucid, I realized how blessed I was, compared to that poor family. I had never known a despair so awful that it prompted me to try to take my life. I do not think I had any sleep at all that night. Like everyone else in ICU, all I could think about was the girl in the bed opposite me, and from the other side of the room I watched her parents weep, the medical staff rush about as they tried to bring her back from the brink, and her motionless body beneath the hospital covers. I have often wondered if that girl got better, and how she is doing now.

I was brought back into surgery the next morning. Thankfully, on the second attempt the procedure went well, and I was released shortly afterwards to start my recovery. I wore a heavy cast for ten weeks, and then a supportive boot for another six weeks. I did my best to be as independent as possible, but obviously I needed a lot of help. I could not drive, so family and friends had to take me everywhere I wanted to go. It was hard for me to cook and clean, so I required a lot of help with that too. As soon as the cast came off, I was in a huge amount of pain and depended on my loved ones for absolutely everything, as I could barely leave the couch. I wondered if the surgery had worked at all, or if I would find that my condition had actually been worsened by the intervention.

I had to have physiotherapy in Drogheda, which was agonizing, but it did help me to gradually regain use of my ankle. All during that period, I had to work quite hard to stay focused on my recovery, and I have to admit that there were times when it was very challenging. I meditated, I did my best to think positively and do my affirmations, and I thought about the future, when I would no longer be in pain and would be visiting my friends, working, and enjoying my life to the full again.

Even with all the support I got from my parents, sister, and other friends and family members, I was acutely aware of how vulnerable I was as I slowly recovered. Something as simple as having a shower was quite complicated, because I could not get my cast wet; I figured out a way to do it involving plastic bags, duct tape and a lot of hopping. Ultimately, though, the pain and the many months of recuperation were worth it, as my ankle healed well. It was such a relief that the surgery was a success, because I had started to become genuinely frightened that I might end up having to use a wheelchair, which was a prospect that I dreaded.

When I was finally discharged from treatment, the doctors said that they were pleased with my progress, but warned me that the good results were only going to be temporary, because the way I walk puts huge pressure on my ankle, and it was only a matter of time before it deteriorated again. All I could do was continue to work hard to stay positive and hope that it would last for as long as possible. So far, my ankle is hanging in there.

With that out of the way, I was ready to move on to another job, and this time I fancied something different. Although I had only just regained my ability to walk properly, I signed up for a beauty specialist diploma – make-up, nails, facials, skincare, waxing, customer service, and so forth. It was a very steep learning curve for me, as I had never worked in that area before, and while I might have thought that I enjoyed cosmetics and putting them on, I quickly realized how little I actually knew, and that beauty therapy was actually much more complex than I imagined. I enjoyed the course very much, and started to feel confident that I would like working in the field.

On graduating, I immediately found work at a place in

Drogheda that offered facials and make-up services, and also sold products directly to customers. I fitted in there very quickly, largely because the other staff members were so lovely and went out of their way to make me feel welcome. I was soon firm friends with Ruth, who is one of my best friends to this day, and with our colleagues Emma, Kim and Elsie. They were all quite a lot younger than me, but that was no barrier to our friendship. Drogheda, I soon learned, was a very welcoming town. As I had grown up in Dublin, I knew nobody there, but within weeks of starting work in the town centre, I felt as though I had been there for years, as the people I passed each day on my way to and from the salon recognized me and began to say hello.

I had always been keenly aware of how much women are judged on their appearance – probably more aware than most women are, because it is so difficult for me to find clothes that fit me and look good and because of my lingering self-consciousness about my scars and the shape of my body. Working in the cosmetics industry showed me that carefully applied make-up can do wonders for someone's self-esteem and that it can be downright therapeutic at times. Sure, of course it would be nicer to live in a world in which women are not judged in those ways and in which everyone understands that what is on the inside is what counts. But the fact is that we do not live in that world – we live in this one. And in this one, having the right foundation and the right lipstick can give a woman the confidence she needs to get out there and do her thing, because she knows that if she does not present her best face to the world, there are plenty of people who will find fault with her.

I soon built up a client base of my own and got to know some of the people who came in regularly quite well, as we chatted and exchanged news while I did their facials, eye-brows and make-up. There is something so intimate and informal about doing another woman's face that it is easy to share even quite personal stories with someone you only know in that context. I learned a lot about my clients' lives, and they learned a lot about mine. I learned about their hopes for themselves, and the image that they wanted to project to the world, and I helped them to achieve their goals and man-age their expectations when they came in asking for a treatment or a look that I knew would not suit them.

I remember one customer coming in very upset, because she had given birth recently, and the hormonal fluctuations had made her skin break out in a rash. On top of the lack of sleep and the emotional rush of caring for her newborn, looking in the mirror and seeing her spots was just more than she could bear, when all she wanted was to look beautiful in her baby's first photographs. I was so happy to be able to offer her some products that would help and ended up doing her face for her and showing her how to use them. We had a lovely chat and, when I had finished and she saw her face in the mirror, she gave me a delighted hug. She left the shop looking amazing, with a spring in her step that had not been there when she came in.

One of the highlights of the year for the business was working at the Electric Picnic music festival, when we set up a mobile make-up studio in a converted camper van so that festival-goers could have their make-up done and braids put in their hair. As you can imagine, the pace was absolutely hectic and it could be tough keeping everything under con-trol. It was always huge fun, and we were always completely exhausted by the end of it.

As well as applying clients' make-up, whether in-store or

at the Electric Picnic, ours was a retail business that sold cosmetics to the general public. I gained a lot of experience in retail, and in how to keep the shop fully stocked and looking clean, inviting and professional to anyone who came in. At the store, we did our best to welcome all our customers and make them see that we really appreciated their business and that we would bend over backwards to help them find the product they were looking for.

The irony was that the shop did not stock any foundations or powders that I could use on my skin, so all the while I was recommending this or that product to the customers coming in, my own skin was bare. The fact that there was no foundation for me was a bit of a running joke among the staff. The products for people with olive or Mediterranean complexions were not right for me, and at first we had none at all for people of colour. When Black or Asian people came to the shop to buy cosmetics, we often had to tell them that we had nothing for them. If they wanted a makeover, or to have their make-up done for a special occasion, we would have to ask them to bring their own foundation and powder. They were all used to this situation, although I found it extremely embarrassing, and they never got annoyed or upset, but I felt bad about not being able to treat all of our customers the same. Eventually my boss sourced a limited range of shades for people of colour and we mixed and matched them as necessary.

Working in the cosmetics business really brought home to me the fact that when you are part of a minority, people often do not think of you at all. Obviously, most people in Ireland are white, so it just makes sense for a cosmetics store to stock a wide range of foundations and powders to suit the various shades of white skin. Nobody (or at least nobody reasonable) is going to deliberately exclude people with dark skin just to be mean – but a lot of people will simply never think of providing cosmetics for them, because it will never even cross their mind.

It is very disheartening for people with darker skin to go shopping for a little make-up only to find that there is nothing that suits them at all, and that 'nude' tones will never include them. By the late 2010s, bigger outlets were beginning to cater more for people with dark skin, but most places in Ireland simply did not consider them as potential customers. It was not really anyone's fault, because it is actually very difficult for a small company like the one I worked for to stock a full range of products; it was just the way it was. But, at the same time, it was another reminder that people like me can be seen as an aberration, a deviation from the norm, and just not catered for at all, or experienced as awkward when we simply ask to be given the same treatment as everybody else.

I loved my job at the shop, and eventually rose to the position of store manager, but as the years passed, I was beginning to feel a little restless. Additionally, that sort of work is much tougher than you might think. Make-up artists are on their feet and active all day long. It is not just skilled work; it is very physically demanding. Make-up artists often have to work through the weekends and during annual holiday periods too, so it can be hard to maintain a decent work–life balance. Although I had grown used to standing up all day, I wanted to move on – but having changed career path dramatically a couple of times already, I didn't know what I wanted to do next, and did not feel like leaving my job without a clear plan or a vision for the future. I hoped that life would intervene and show me the way.

10. Out of Breath

The weather was miserable in October 2015, so I was not surprised when I got a bad cold. I took care of myself for a few days, waiting to see if it would go away, and then when it turned into a serious cough instead of getting better, I made an appointment and went to the doctor.

Because my lungs do not have the space they need to expand the way they should, I have always been very prone to colds and lung infections, and going to the doctor is just part of the routine for me. Since turning thirty-five, I had become aware that my colds, infections and visits to the doctor were becoming gradually more frequent and that it was taking me longer to get over each one. I was increasingly tired and breathless in the evenings when I got in from work. I did not want to think about the implications of this, so I just carried on with my life and continued dealing with the infections and viruses one at a time. Mam was worried about me, and kept telling me that I was working too hard, but I brushed her concerns away, and told her that I was absolutely fine.

Now, the doctor confirmed that I had an infection and gave me some antibiotics that she was sure would take care of it. She told me not to overdo things and to make sure that I was eating well and getting plenty of sleep. After a couple of days on the antibiotics, I felt a little better, so I continued to go to work and to get on with my normal life. As the weeks passed, things were getting busier and busier in the shopping centre where I worked – everyone was doing their Christmas shopping, and a lot of women were buying new make-up for the festive season. My cough was still bothering me, so I went back to the doctor and she gave me another antibiotic.

By early December, I was still coughing, but felt well enough to go to work, although I was exhausted from lack of sleep, as the cough, which was often associated with a horrible sensation of panic and claustrophobia, was keeping me up half the night. Because I felt more comfortable propped up, I was spending hours during the night under my duvet on the sofa, watching television until I finally managed to sleep.

I worked right up to Christmas Eve and then enjoyed the usual hectic Christmas Day with my family. I was working on Stephen's Day, and the next day, the 27th, I had promised Ciara and Dave that I would stay with the boys while they hit the sales.

'Are you sure you're OK to mind them?' Ciara asked. 'You don't want a break?'

'I'll be grand,' I said. 'Sure, I'd be only sitting at home anyway.'

Jamie was busy with his new video game and Charlie and I watched a kids' movie together. It was lovely to be with my nephews, but I felt oddly detached from the experience.

A few hours later, Ciara and Dave came back with their shopping. They had bought a few bits and pieces for me, and Ciara said that she would help me bring them out to the car when it was time for me to go. Dave made dinner in the kitchen and called us in to have it.

I sat on the sofa and looked at the open double doors that connected the living room to the kitchen. The walk to the kitchen was a distance of just a few metres, but it suddenly seemed terribly far away, and I felt exhausted just thinking about it.

Ciara looked at me sharply.

'Marguerite,' she said, 'you're not well, are you?'

'What?' I said. 'No, I'm grand.'

'Your breathing is all over the place,' Ciara said, her voice full of concern. 'You sound like you can't catch your breath at all.'

'I'm grand,' I said again. 'I'm just tired after Christmas.'

I managed to get up off the sofa and shuffled into the kitchen for my tea. Dave had put out plates with the dinner on them. I looked at my fork and realized that I did not have the strength to pick it up. I could barely even lift my hand from the table.

'You're not well at all,' Ciara said decisively. 'I'm not happy about it. I'm going to ring the cottage hospital and get you an appointment.'

The cottage hospital is a small medical centre near the Lourdes Hospital in Drogheda that serves as a sort of out-of-hours emergency service for the broader community.

'I'll be grand,' I said again to Ciara. 'If I don't feel well tomorrow, I'll ring them then.'

Despite my repeated assurances, Ciara could see I was anything but grand. She put her foot down and rang the triage nurse, who said that she would ring back and speak with me directly.

When the nurse came on the line a few minutes later, I was coughing so hard, and finding it so difficult to catch my breath, I could not even talk to her. I handed the receiver back to Ciara and she made an appointment with the nurse for later that evening. I wanted to drive home then, but Ciara said that I was not well enough, and Dave dropped me home. They rang Dad and arranged for him to bring me to the appointment. He picked me up on time and helped me into the car.

'I'm fine, Dad,' I said between coughs. 'Ciara's just being cautious.'

Dad said that it was better to be safe than sorry.

The hospital waiting room was overheated and uncomfortable and I fidgeted on the hard plastic chair, waiting to be seen. I remember feeling quite dazed and confused, as though nothing around me was completely real. When the triage nurse called me in, she checked my vitals and then looked at me kindly.

'Do you realize how laboured your breathing is?' she said. 'You're really struggling to breathe.'

'Am I?' I said vaguely. 'I don't think so.'

I felt as though I was having a dream.

'I'm getting you an appointment with the doctor straight away.'

The doctor took one look at me.

'Marguerite,' she said, 'you're going to have to go into the hospital.'

I nodded. They wanted to give me another antibiotic, I thought, only for some reason they were not able to write me the prescription here and I had to go to the hospital to get it. That was OK.

'We need to get you on oxygen without delay,' the doctor said.

'OK,' I said.

I allowed the doctor and nurse to lead me to a gurney at the back of the clinic, where they laid me down and put an oxygen mask on me. The nurse bent over me with a reassuring smile.

'I'm just going to go out and talk to your dad,' she said. 'You should find it a bit easier to breathe with the oxygen and I think you'll feel more comfortable soon.'

I was indeed starting to feel a little better with the oxygen, and when Dad came in looking all worried, I felt guilty about making him feel bad.

'Are you OK, love?' he asked.

'I'm grand,' I reassured him. 'I feel much better now.'

Dad asked if he could drive me to the main hospital himself, but we were told that I needed to be brought by ambulance, so that I could be admitted for treatment at once. I was mortified. I thought that the paramedics in the ambulance would see that I was not really very sick, and feel angry with me for being a hypochondriac and taking a bed that should have been kept for someone with a real problem.

'Will you stop worrying?' said Dad. 'If they called an ambulance for you then you must need it.'

Dad rang Mam to tell her that I was being admitted to hospital. She wanted to come up immediately, but I told him to tell her not to, that I would be grand and there was no point in making a fuss.

I remember sitting in the ambulance while the medics took my stats. They brought me into the hospital and put me in the emergency bed, all hooked up to the oxygen and everything else. The hospital was frantically busy, and it took the doctors about an hour to get to me. I was sure that they would say that the cottage hospital had overreacted and that I could go home now, but instead they said that they wanted to keep me in overnight for monitoring.

I looked down at my feet and realized that I had put on odd socks that morning, and that I had worn them all day without even noticing. That is something I would never do,

151

and I freaked out when Dad came back in, having followed the ambulance up to the hospital in his car.

'What will the doctors think when they see my odd socks?' I asked him. 'They'll think I'm mad. I need to go home to change.'

'The doctors aren't going to care what socks you have on, Marguerite!' said Dad.

'Dad,' I said, 'I really don't feel well.'

It sounds crazy, but seeing those odd socks was the one thing that made me comprehend that something really was seriously wrong. Still, I thought that there was no point in Dad getting exhausted. I told him to go home. I had my phone, I said, and I would ring him if I needed anything. Somewhat reluctantly, Dad left.

I spent the night in A & E, during the course of which various people came to take blood samples and check how I was getting on. I remember feeling so tired that I did not have the slightest interest in any of it. The oxygen masks at the hospital did not fit me properly because I am so small, so they arranged to have a child's mask delivered from Temple Street Children's Hospital in Dublin.

Anyone can get a chest infection, and anyone can get so sick that they go into respiratory failure, but the dice were loaded against me because of my scoliosis. When I get an infection in my lungs, it can be extremely resistant to treatment. I could easily have had a latent infection for months, or even years, before I finally crashed and ended up in hospital.

My condition remained poor that night, despite all the treatments I was receiving. Outside in the corridor the next morning, one of the nurses pulled Dad aside.

'You should know,' she said, 'that you have a very, very sick daughter.'

'She's been a bit under the weather for a while,' Dad said. 'She's had a cold that's dragged on and she's coughing a bit.'

'No,' said the nurse. 'She's not "a bit under the weather". She's extremely unwell.'

At about midnight on the 28th, my second night in the hospital, I was moved to the intensive care unit, because my breathing was continuing to deteriorate. Although I was quite confused, I remember thinking that it was just like being in a medical show on TV as I was pushed through the doors into an ICU cubicle filled with clicking and beeping machines.

I lay passively in my bed, meekly allowing people to do things to me – stick needles in my arm, adjust the flow of the oxygen, take my blood pressure. I had no inkling of how sick I was, or not until one of the young women who used to come to the cosmetics shop to buy her make-up appeared in the ward with tea and toast. She recognized me immediately, and the colour drained right out of her face.

'That's Marguerite!' she said. 'I know her from the shop.'

I waved at her and said hello, and she smiled weakly, but I could see that she was seriously freaked out. For the first time, I began to think that maybe this was more than I could handle.

Back at home, Mam and Dad were concerned about me, but they had been reassured that I should start feeling much better now that I had an oxygen mask that fitted me and were hopeful that there would be a positive change by the morning.

When Mam rang the hospital first thing on the 29th, the doctors told her that they had not managed to stabilize my condition and that they were going to have to intubate me, as I was no longer able to breathe on my own. From this point on, my own memories are hazy and confused, and sometimes completely absent, and I have had to rely on my family's accounts.

Of course, Mam and Dad rang Ciara to let her know what was happening, and then they rushed to the hospital, with Ciara saying that she would follow them up shortly. When they got there, they were brought to ICU, where initially they could only see me through the glass doors that gave on to my room. I had already been intubated because the medics could not wait any longer. I lay, unconscious, in a huge bed with a vast array of machinery behind me that was monitoring my oxygen levels and everything that was going on in my body. The medical team explained that I was not well enough to make decisions on my own behalf, so my family would have to do it for me. If I did not begin responding to the treatment, they might be asked to make the very difficult decision about withdrawing it and letting nature take its course.

'She's going into respiratory failure,' they said. 'We're doing our best, but you should start to prepare yourselves . . . and contact anyone who would like to see her while there's still time. You will need to get her affairs in order. We are very worried about her.'

'But she's going to be OK?' Mam asked. 'She'll start getting better soon?'

The doctor just shook his head slowly from side to side. Mam felt like she was going to fall over, and she grabbed on to Dad to hold herself up. She told the doctors that I had been at work the day before I got sick; it was very difficult for her to get her head around the idea that I could have been at work one day and so ill the next.

'She can't possibly have been working,' one of the doctors said. 'Her oxygen levels are far too low. There's no way she would have been able to get up and walk around, let alone work.'

'She was,' Mam insisted. 'She hates taking a day off work.'

Later, Mam told me that this was the moment she truly realized that I was seriously ill. She was terrified that the hospital staff would underestimate me because I am so small and can look very frail to anyone who does not know me as well as she does. Her fear was that, if my condition deteriorated, they would assume I was not going to be strong enough to fight to stay alive, and they might not try all they possibly could to help me get well again.

'Please don't give up on her,' Mam urged the medical team. 'She's stronger than she looks. She's a real fighter.'

Ciara had arrived at the car park, and Mam and Dad had the horrible task of telling her how desperate the situation was. They were so emotionally exhausted by this stage that they were no longer able to answer the doctors' questions, so Ciara took over when she reached ICU. She explained that we didn't know what illnesses ran on either side of my birth parents, that I had been adopted as a small child and we never had access to that sort of information. She shared as much as she could about the various health issues that I had had over the years.

The doctors and nurses warned my family that I would probably look unconscious when they went to visit me, because I was very weak and heavily sedated in the induced coma that they had put me in, but it was likely I would be able to hear them and it would be good for me to know that my loved ones were there and to listen to them speaking to me.

'Just positive talk when you're in there,' they said. 'Say whatever you can to reassure Marguerite that we are doing everything in our power to make her well.'

Ciara insisted that Mam and Dad ring Auntie Angela, Uncle David and my cousin Gary, who has always been such a close friend of mine, ever since he came into our lives when I was five years old.

Then Ciara entered my ICU room and stood beside my bed.

'You're doing great, sis!' she said, looking down at me and holding my hand.

I heard every word, but because I was intubated and sedated, and because I was so weak, I was not really able to react. With huge effort, I opened my eyes and looked up at her. I blinked, and then I closed my eyes again. I think I was trying to tell Ciara that I could hear her, and that I was going to be OK.

At some point after Ciara's visit, I woke up – or at least I thought I did – and saw, as clear as day, two big, grey wolves sitting on either side of me, with a huge angel hovering above, looking down, its vast wings reaching the ceiling and touching down towards the floor. Whether it was the drugs I was on, my oxygen-starved mind doing its best to comfort me, or an actual vision, I will never know – but I interpreted what I saw as a sign that I was indeed going to come through this, that I was going to survive.

While I lay there, largely oblivious to what was going on, Mam, Dad, Ciara, Auntie Angela, Uncle David and my cousin Gary gathered in the Costa coffee shop nearby. Auntie Angela and Uncle David wanted to support us all in any way they could. They had seen me through the glass doors of my room, but had not been allowed in. Then they had all been told by the hospital staff to take a break and have a cup of tea and something to eat because they would need to take care of themselves if they were going to be there for me. But nobody felt like eating. Auntie Angela and Uncle David were struggling to understand how I could have become so unwell so quickly. Ciara told me afterwards that they were all crying, so upset that they did not care who could see them.

Much to everyone's surprise, I regained consciousness on my own later that day. I understood that I was in hospital, but I was extremely confused about what was going on. I will never forget the noise of the ventilator breathing for me, or the sensation of the vibrations in my chest. Because I was intubated, I obviously could not speak, so I gestured to the nurse to bring me some paper and a pen – but when she did, I could not remember how to write or spell out words. I was on so much medication that I was very baffled about what was happening and could not always remember who had come in to see me and who had not.

Ten days later, I was still intubated, as well as being fed through a tube, with the exception of a brief period on New Year's Eve when they had tried me without the ventilator to see how I would cope – not well, it turned out; I lasted just a little while until breathing suddenly became impossible and I was put on the machine again. I vaguely remember those days. I remained heavily sedated to keep me still and calm, but I was awake a lot of the time, although very confused. Sometimes I was able to communicate with my family by writing in a notebook that Mam had brought in for me, and sometimes I thought that I was holding a pen and writing notes to them, but I was just waving my hands in the air. Often the notes that I did write were gibberish, although I was sure that I was making perfect sense. I remember being very concerned about my mortgage and wanting to be sure that it would get paid, even though I was not working. At times I managed to meditate and to keep my mind focused on anything other than my illness; at other times I just lay there in a daze, struggling to understand what was happening.

A lot of people find being intubated unbearable and try to tear out the tube, even though they are sedated. But I coped with it very well and seemed comfortable, despite being awake or semi-awake a good bit of the time. My doctors were concerned that I was too comfortable with it in and that my body might simply forget how to breathe on its own. Eventually, they decided that it was time to take out the ventilator, hopefully for good. Mam was visiting that day and they outlined the situation to her.

'She can't stay intubated for the rest of her life,' they said.

They explained that, if necessary, they would do a tracheotomy to help me to breathe. They also said that they were actually surprised that I was still alive, because most patients in the condition that I had been in would not have survived.

'I told you,' Mam said to them. 'Don't be fooled by appearances. This one is as strong as an ox.'

I was just alert enough to know that I did not want a tracheotomy, and furiously shook my head, but Mam and Ciara had to make the call and sign their permission for the intervention to be carried out if it was needed. First, they asked the anaesthetist to speak to me to make sure that I understood and that I accepted what might happen. After listening to her, I agreed to have a tracheotomy if I really needed one.

On the day when I was due to start breathing on my own, Mam was told to go for lunch and that, when she came back, she could be there when my tube was removed. While she was away, the anaesthetist gradually lowered my sedation levels until I was fully conscious and aware of what was going on. A horrible sensation of nausea came over me, and

I was sure that I was going to vomit and then choke, because the breathing tube was blocking the way. I panicked, but because I could not speak, I alerted the anaesthetist by banging my phone against the edge of the bed. When she came to me, I managed to type *I feel nauseous* into the phone.

Suddenly, there was a whole medical team around me. The nurse held my hand and told me to look at her and do what she said. I had to cough when they told me to while another nurse was prepared to suction me if I did get sick. In seconds, the tube was gone and I was lying there, breathing on my own for the first time in days.

'Well?' somebody asked.

I was not able to talk at first, so I did a thumbs-up. The whole team broke out into applause, huge smiles on all of their faces. I remember lying on the bed looking up at them. My medical team, like the hospital staff in general, were from all over the world. There were nurses, doctors and anaesthetists from places like Nigeria, the Philippines, Thailand and Poland. Over the course of a single day in hospital, I listened to accents of all sorts. The various members of the team all looked very different from one another – but as I started to take my first independent breaths since I had been intubated, they all wore identical huge smiles and I could see that, while taking care of me was their job, they were also genuinely happy for me.

The ventilator had given my lungs the time they needed to get better, and finally I was on the mend. My throat was so sore, I felt as though I had swallowed gravel, but knowing that I could breathe on my own at last was the best sensation in the world, and I was happy to have a sore throat, as I knew it was only because the doctors had done all they could to make me well – and it had worked.

Mam, who had gone for lunch, had missed it all – which I am glad about now, because I think it would have been very traumatic for her seeing me go through all that. She was back at my bedside after lunch and, although talking was still painful and difficult, I was able to say a few words to her. She beamed at me in joy and relief because she and I both knew that I had turned a corner, and that the doctors' worst fears for me were not going to be realized.

'I'm after missing the moment they took out the tube!' Mam said. 'I wanted to be there for you.'

When I was younger, Mam had been there for hundreds of my medical procedures, and I know that each one was a terrible ordeal for her. At least on this occasion she had arrived in time to see that I was getting better, without having to witness what had happened before.

'Mam, I can talk!' I said.

My voice was small, hoarse and reedy, but it was amazing to say anything at all, after all that time on the ventilator.

That night the trauma of everything that had happened finally hit me, and I became deeply depressed and lost all interest in speaking to anyone. I worried that I would never work again, or maybe never even walk again, and that I would not be able to live as an independent adult, as I was used to doing. There was a new nurse on the ward and she became concerned, because she had been told that I was a live wire who interacted as best I could with the staff, and she was seeing a patient who was the exact opposite – withdrawn, inert and morose. Bless her, when Mam rang to check on me, the nurse said that she felt I was not doing well, judging by how I was behaving. Mam asked her to find out if I wanted her to visit, and I said that I did, despite the late hour.

As soon as Mam arrived, I dissolved into floods of

helpless tears. I remember needing her as much then, at the age of forty-one, as I had needed her when I was a little girl in Crumlin Children's Hospital, struggling to understand what was happening to me. To tell the truth, I think that I was reacting not just to what had been happening to me recently, but also to long-repressed memories of that awful time, and perhaps even to deep-rooted memories of my very early childhood that I cannot consciously recall. That night I fell asleep holding Mam's hand, as though I was still the little girl whom she had taken home from the mother and baby home, many years before.

Dad, and then Ciara, came in the morning, and once again I could not cope with the flood of emotions I experienced, and burst into tears. I was worried that I was going mad, or that I was being a nuisance to the medical staff, and wondered why I could not channel the positivity that I usually feel, but the nurse on duty – Cherry, a lovely woman from the Philippines – said that everything I was experiencing was perfectly normal, that these were symptoms of PTSD, and that they were relieved I was expressing my emotions at last, as I had been on a high until now, and had not shed a tear. What I was going through was not just normal, she said, but healthy. I had been through a huge trauma, and if I did not allow myself to process my negative feelings now, I would be at elevated risk later for psychological problems relating to my experiences.

'To be honest,' Cherry said, 'we were getting worried about you. I know that it's hard, but this is much better than going home and crashing later. You need to start dealing with what has happened, and you need to give yourself a little time to work through it all.'

After that, the nurses on my ward went out of their way to

be kind and supportive of me. They encouraged me to express my feelings about what had happened, and said that, if I ever needed it, the hospital could offer me therapy to help me come to terms with it all. I did not reject the idea of therapy, but at the time I was so focused on getting physically better I was not really able to think about anything but getting back on my feet again. I think I was afraid that if I stopped for a moment to ponder how difficult it had all been, it would just be too much for me. I knew that I needed to be strong.

A day or two after the tube was taken out of my throat, my consultant gave my family a talking-to, saying that I had to face facts and that working was likely to be too much for me in the future because I would probably never be the same again. He said that I should consider giving up the idea of a career and that I would qualify for a disability pension. It was kinder, he explained, to be realistic about what my prospects were. It would be better than letting me raise my expectations only for them to be dashed by reality.

Mam repeated to me a version of the doctor's advice. I said no without even having to think about it. Weak as I felt at that time, this was a step too far for me. I have always loved working, and while I am not out there curing cancer or discovering new galaxies, or anything like that, I have always done my best to work hard and to bring all I can to the job. Getting up in the morning, going to work and doing the best I can is one of my most important sources of strength, because it reminds me, every day, that I have the right to live my life to the full. I could not imagine spending the rest of my life at home. What would I do? How would I fill my days? What would be the point?

The physiotherapist came to see me to give advice on how to get moving again.

'We'll start by getting you sitting up by yourself,' he said. 'That'll be a good place to begin.'

I thought that sitting up was going to be great, as he set up a comfy chair with lots of cushions and a blanket beside the bed. When he lifted me up in the bed, it was very awkward, as I was so weak and had so many tubes and things attached to me. I decided that I did not really want to get out of bed, but I said nothing. As soon as the physio had settled me into place, I realized that I did not even have the strength to hold myself up while sitting and I felt extremely weak and vulnerable. It reminded me of when I was little and needed a plaster cast just to sit up. I started to slide down, and the physio had to grab me to save me from landing on the floor. I was relieved when I was finally put back into bed again, where I felt safe and protected under the covers, although I was glad that Mam was there and that she had seen me sitting up, at least for a little while.

What if this is as good as it gets? I wondered as I lay under the hospital blankets. Am I going to spend the rest of my life depending on other people for everything?

After a month in hospital, the doctors considered me well enough to be discharged into my parents' care. I was thrilled to be able to leave at last, but worried about how we were all going to cope. I know that I still looked awful the day I was allowed home. I had had so many needles stuck in me, and so many tubes connected to me, that I looked like a heroin addict, my arms riddled with puncture marks and bruises. My usually thin thighs were swollen with water retention, and I had lost weight. Because a central line had been placed in my neck, I had barely been able to move the whole time I was in hospital, and all of my muscles had weakened from lack of use. I was so frail, I was sent home with a Zimmer frame, but at first I was not even strong enough to use that, and Dad carried me to and from the bathroom and my bedroom whenever I needed to go anywhere.

I needed a lot of care for the first two months of my recovery, as I gradually taught my muscles how to work again, and slowly got back to some kind of normality. It was hard to stay positive about the future, but somehow I managed to focus on the idea of getting better and, little by little, I regained my strength. I used all the tools that I had at my disposal – my normally positive outlook on life, my knowledge of meditation, my close relationships with family and friends – to stay in the moment. Life was going to go on, I realized, although perhaps not in exactly the same way as before.

Very few people in my life know how difficult that time was for me – not the illness, so much, because I was so sick that I did not even know what was happening – but the aftermath when, for the first time as an adult, I truly confronted the reality of my physical frailty and accepted that I do have a disability that impacts on me in all sorts of ways. All of my life, Mam and Dad had encouraged me to do exactly the same things as everyone else. We all knew that I might need to do some things in a slightly different way to other people, but I had always managed to achieve whatever I set out to do. My illness and the long time I spent on the respirator was a cruel reminder that everyone has their limits – and perhaps I had just been faced with mine.

Maybe it was the fact that I needed to be carried like a baby, or perhaps it was the aftermath of the trauma, but this difficult time was a milestone for me in more ways than one. As I started to get better, I felt that I was being reborn – that I should take what had happened to me as a message that it was time to make some big changes in my life. Time to confront some of my most painful realities, including the fact that my recent illness had left me physically weaker and more vulnerable than before. Time to use all that I had learned to make a difference in the world. The question was, how?

11. Searching for Answers

I forced myself to go back to work about three months after getting out of hospital, and only two or three weeks after starting to be able to walk around the house, still with the aid of the Zimmer frame. My boss was very nervous about my return. She worried that I might not be strong enough, and that I could have a setback. For the first three weeks, at her suggestion, I did office work and admin at the business's warehouse. After that, I went back to the shop. I think that each and every one of us knew I should not be there, and my colleagues went out of their way to support me and make things as easy as possible, but I was terrified that if I took too much sick leave, I might never get back to work at all. I did not want to lose the personal independence that is so central to my self-identity and to how I live. I did not want people to see me as helpless or weak. Above all, I did not want to see myself that way.

It was tough at first, but by the summer of that year, I was working full-time again and doing my best to pretend that my recent hospital experience had never happened. Sometimes people tried to talk to me about my illness and my difficult recovery, but I always changed the subject, partly because I did not want them to think of me as ill or disabled, but mostly because I did not trust myself to talk about that terrible episode without breaking down.

At the time, I thought that I was just getting on with things, but looking back now I can see that my rush back to work was at least partly about avoiding a confrontation between the life I wanted for myself, and the reality, which was that I had so nearly lost everything. By keeping busy, I could stay focused on the present and future, and try not to think about my illness at all. While the time would come to examine that awful period in more depth, back then I was making the best decision for myself and keeping myself as safe as I could, the only way I knew how.

So, for the first year and a half after my near-death experience, I pretended to myself, and to everybody else, that I was completely fine, although I did not consciously realize what I was doing. I just kept my head down and got on with work. I saw my friends whenever I could, and kept up with my social life. I decided to share my apartment with a friend. We soon got into a rhythm and became excellent housemates. When my friend Paige needed to find a home for a dog, a little Pomeranian called Mia joined the household too. Having grown up with dogs, I was thrilled to have one of my own and loved the way little Mia lived in the moment, always excited about the things going on around her.

Eventually, though, despite surrounding myself with supportive friends and family members, and despite keeping myself as busy as possible at all times, I had to start dealing with the reality of what had happened. Even the beeping sound of machines in a hospital drama on TV made my heart race and gave me huge anxiety, to the extent that I would have to change the channel and do some deep breathing to calm myself down. It became impossible to ignore the fact that, no matter how strong I am or would like to be, I was still living with trauma that was far from resolved.

In the process of beginning to accept my own frailties, I allowed a space in my mind to open and admit the possibility that I was still dealing with another type of trauma too, relating to the way in which I came into the world, the very early years of my life – most of which I have no conscious memory of – and the way in which I have been forced to live with no knowledge of my biological parents. Knowing that I had come so close to dying, without ever having found out about them, made me keenly aware of how much I wanted to learn the truth, while at the same time realizing that, no matter what I do, I might never learn it at all, and that I may have to figure out a way for that to be OK.

Although she did not know the extent of what I was going through, Mam could see that I was struggling a little, and I know that she was quite worried about me at that time. Ever since my stay in hospital, she had been suggesting that it might be a good idea for me to have some therapy to help me deal with my feelings about what had happened. But because I was not yet ready to face all of these difficult thoughts and emotions, I left them on the back burner and waited. I told Mam that if I ever felt that therapy was necessary, I would organize it myself. I reminded her that I have been through countless challenges in the past, and that I have always come back smiling. I reassured her that I had everything under control and that I knew what I was doing. Gently, but quite firmly, I was telling Mam to trust me, that I would be able to deal with everything in my own way.

Meditation had always been a big help for me and very much took the place of therapy. I have always regretted the fact that – because of my scoliosis – I am not able to do sports and unwind through physical activity, but I did find that meditation provided me with a way to unwind after work that seemed to help me as a ten-kilometre run helps someone else, and so I joined a meditation group in Drogheda.

The group was friendly and open, and there was something really special about meditating with other like-minded people. They practised mantra chanting, and I loved it – I was a bit self-conscious at first, but soon I was chanting along with everyone else, and when I left after each session I was full of energy and feeling recharged. So, when the opportunity to visit India with the group came up, I decided to go.

Visiting India was an absolutely extraordinary experience. Fifty people travelled from Ireland, and from the moment we got off the plane in Delhi and were given our flower garlands, it was one sensory overload after another. We were bussed to a number of locations, mostly in the Himalayas, and we visited several temples, where we could meditate and chant alongside the locals. We often had no language in common with the people we met, but we were still able to communicate with one another through the universal language of chanting and meditation. It was a very moving reminder of the shared humanity that brings people together, even when at a glance they can seem to be very different. I think that everyone in our group was changed by their experiences on that trip; it certainly changed me. One of the other travellers was a woman called Sarah Richardson. We clicked immediately and have been good friends ever since. Sarah practises reiki, and I finished my training with her, becoming a master and meditation teacher, so I am now qualified to teach reiki as well as lead meditation groups.

After working in the beauty industry for five years, and having reached a managerial position, about two years after my health crisis business slowed down in our shopping centre – partly because so much retail was being shifted online – and once again I was made redundant. This was upsetting as I had enjoyed the work, had loved working

alongside my colleagues, and was very aware of how return-
ing to the workplace after being ill had been a lifeline for me;
also of how accommodating my boss had been of my additional needs then. At the same time, a part of me was grateful,
at first, for the break, because it had been a very eventful few
years, and apart from when I had been too sick to work, I had
taken very little time off. That gratitude lasted for a few days,
by which stage I was bored and fed up of being at home, and
missing my colleagues and friends at work badly.

I signed on for the Jobseeker's Allowance and started
applying for a new job straight away because I absolutely
hated being without work. I was very grateful to live in a
country that has a safety net for people who are between
jobs, but I was determined not to be on state benefits for a
single minute longer than necessary. I loathed waking up in
the morning and not knowing what I would do all day. I had
a mortgage to think about, and worried that I would run into
financial difficulties if I could not make the monthly pay-
ments. My friends advised me to take it easy for a while, to
enjoy the unexpected time off, but I am not the sort of person who likes putting her feet up. I started to panic about
how I was going to fill my days until I found a new job.
Everyone asked me what sort of work I wanted to do next,
but I did not have a clue. With my varied experience of
admin, retail, management and the beauty industry, I just
applied for everything I was qualified to do, and more. I was
hopeful that something would turn up soon.

My job search was not helped by the fact that I had been
strongly advised by my doctors to keep my commute to an
absolute minimum, and that I should take a job in which I
would never be required to travel. They said that if I insisted
on working, the least I could do to protect my health was to

work as locally as possible, so that I did not have to face a gruelling journey as well as a hard day at the office. That meant that I needed to think in terms of finding a job that would not involve driving an hour or more to get there and back.

After almost a year without work, I was starting to get very anxious about the future, and extremely frustrated with all the employers who advertised for applicants and then did not even bother to contact them to let them know that they were not interested, not even sending an autoreply. As usual, I was meditating every day, and the peace of mind that meditation brought me helped me to cope with this very difficult time. I used positive affirmations too, telling myself firmly that everything happens for a reason, and that the universe must want me to take this time off to reframe and learn. But while the positive affirmations did help me, I started to think that I might never find another job again and worried that, if that happened, I might become depressed and withdrawn.

My family were worried about me too, although I was doing my best to put on a brave face for them. They know that it has always been very important for me to be independent, and I am sure they were concerned that, if my jobless spell persisted, it would start to have a serious impact on my mental and emotional health. They all did their best to keep my spirits up, even as I waited fruitlessly for a response to my latest round of job applications.

Then I spotted an advertisement for admin staff with the VHI, one of Ireland's main private health insurance providers. The clinic was in Swords, a North Dublin suburb near the airport, which was a commutable distance from my home in Bettystown, and I seemed to have plenty of relevant experience. I sent in my CV, and was invited to attend an interview shortly afterwards.

Because I had been out of work for so long, I was very nervous before the interview and keenly aware that, if I did get the job, it would be another completely new start. Fortunately, the women who interviewed me were very friendly and helped to put me at ease. We ended up speaking for about an hour, and when I left the interview room I had a feeling that it had gone well. A couple of days later I was offered the job. Finally, I was back at work. I could not have been happier. I had dinner with my whole family that evening to celebrate the end of my long fallow period, and I remember laughing and talking with them, feeling as though an enormous weight had been lifted from my shoulders after all these months.

My new role was as the first contact that most patients would have with our Swiftcare Clinic when something happened to do with their health. I booked them in for their appointments and talked to them during what were often very difficult times in their lives. It was relatively straight-forward work in some ways, but it could also be challenging, helping people to stay calm and on track when they were so concerned about a health issue. I soon realized that my many experiences of the healthcare system made it easier for me to empathize with what the patients I spoke to were going through. They were experiencing emotions of upset, fright, anxiety, anger, and more. Having been in hospital on multiple occasions, including with serious illness and injury, I knew what they needed, and could choose the right words to reassure them that they were in good hands and that we were on their side.

I was just finishing my fourth and final week of training with the VHI when worrying news about what people had initially assumed was only a problem in China started filtering through. When it became clear that Covid was going to wreak havoc in Ireland too, I was very concerned. Hearing journalists talking about how severely the disease affected the most vulnerable members of society, I knew that they were talking about people like me. For someone like me, with a long and complex medical history, and lungs that are always under stress, Covid would be an awful challenge; and if I were to catch it and die, people who did not know me would comfort themselves with the thought that I had an under-lying condition, and that what had happened to me did not apply to them. I realized that I had to be extremely careful, and decided to inform myself, so I approached one of the doctors at work and asked him what he thought about the pandemic and how it was likely to evolve.

'This is something that is likely to be an issue for a long time,' he said. 'Possibly as much as three or four years. It's definitely not going to go away after a few weeks.'

At that time, the media was pushing the idea that if we all stayed at home for just a few weeks, we would be able to stop the virus from spreading at all. My doctor friend's pessimistic view struck me as a much more likely scenario.

God, I thought. There's no way I could stay at home for three or four years. I'd go mad.

My employers were very helpful. They told me that I would qualify for the pandemic payment from the state if I did not want to continue working, and said that, as I was more vulnerable than average to the virus, they would com-pletely understand my decision and would hold my job for me until I was ready to come back. But having just returned to work after a long period of unemployment that I had found very stressful and difficult, I was aghast at the thought of having to spend another lengthy period at home. I had to take care of my mental as well as my physical health, and I felt that if I could not even go to work, I would crack up.

Once I had confirmed that I wanted to continue working, my employers explained all the measures that they were taking to keep the risk at work to an absolute minimum and reassured me that I would be given all the protection they could provide me with. We would all be very distant from one another, the ventilation system in the office was excellent, and we would all wear our masks at all times. In addition, one of my colleagues and I were given a special room to work in, away from the others.

I was reassured that the company was taking the pandemic so seriously and felt confident that they were doing all they could to keep me and my colleagues safe. While I did wake up some days dreading the thought of having to go to work, considering all that was happening outside, when I actually got in, sat at my desk and got on with my day, I was glad that I was there, and knew that I was very lucky, as a lot of my friends were not able to work and were staying at home, receiving the state Covid payment, and worrying about what was going to happen next. While the situation was quite scary for me, at least I had job security and something to get up for in the mornings.

As the first wave of Covid crashed over Ireland, many of the patients who rang in had contracted the disease, or were very anxious and worried about it. Sometimes they really needed to see a doctor about a health issue that they had, but were so frightened they did not want to leave home. Part of my job was reassuring them that they would be cared for and protected as they received the help they needed. Talking to those patients, who so desperately needed my reassurance, I realized how many people are very alone. I have always been surrounded by family members and friends, and I have always known that there are loads of people in my life who I can count on for help and support. Sometimes I have taken all that for granted, and even assumed that everyone is as fortunate as me; that everyone has people in their lives who are prepared to drop anything to help. Working at the VHI reminded me that I am truly blessed, and that there are a lot of people who, through no fault of their own, have very few loved ones in their lives, and who have to figure things out for themselves when they have a problem or a challenge, or throw themselves on the mercy of strangers.

Because I was born and raised in Dublin, obviously I have a Dublin accent. To the customers phoning the health insurance company, that meant that, to them, I sounded 'white'. Because I have a typical Dublin voice, they just assumed that I am a white Irish woman who looks like them. For some of the patients, this also meant that they felt they could discuss their doctors, nurses and other healthcare providers in ways that they would not if they had realized they were talking to a Black person.

'I couldn't understand a word the foreign doctor said,' they would say, or, 'Does he really have all his qualifications, he must be from Africa?' or, 'You'd just be worried that they wouldn't have the same standards as us,' or, 'I want to see an *Irish* doctor, not a foreigner, can you promise me that?'

Of course, I would reassure them that all of the doctors and nurses were fully trained and experienced. I knew that they were scared and that we can all be cranky and unreasonable when we are scared, and I tried to be understanding, although it was horrible to hear them cast aspersions on the wonderful, highly trained doctors from all over the world who have come to Ireland to take care of us when we are unwell. I would have to bite my tongue to prevent myself from pointing out that our health system would collapse if it were not for the many compassionate and knowledgeable medical staff working in it, or that the world is full of Irish doctors and nurses who have made their careers elsewhere and are themselves the 'foreigners'. Talking to my medical colleagues from overseas, I knew that these attitudes could be annoying and discouraging for them, and I was often amazed by how gracious and tolerant they were in the face of patients who could be nervous, hostile and sometimes even overtly racist when they realized that the person who would be providing them with healthcare was a different colour to themselves.

As the months passed, I was increasingly talking to people who had been ill with Covid, and were now dealing with the lingering after-effects and wondering what the future held for them. The virus waned over the summer, and so did the number of panic-stricken patients ringing the service, but as we entered autumn and started moving towards the Christmas season, the numbers mounted again, and so did public alarm. By December 2020, when the number of people sick with Covid was rising rapidly, along with the numbers dying from the disease, I was becoming more and more concerned about my own health, and started to wonder if I should take some time off, even though I knew that it would do my head in.

Should I be here at all? I asked myself. Am I just pushing myself too far? Am I taking a stupid risk that I'll only regret later on?

I weighed the situation up again and decided that it was still better for me to go to work, where the environment was tightly controlled and my colleagues were medical staff who understood the situation better than anyone, than to stay at home in my apartment, where eventually I would become miserable and unmotivated. I had already spent so much time at home while I was looking for work.

While I remained busy at work throughout the pandemic, I knew that the biggest risk to my health, and to that of my family, was meeting them. As we are all so close, and so sociable, this was very challenging for us. Usually, I saw Mam and Dad, and often Ciara, almost every day, and now we were just talking on the phone. Like everyone, I spent countless hours at home, following the lockdown regulations. My flatmate and my little dog Mia kept me company, but it was hard sometimes, not seeing family and friends and having to rely so much on my own resources to keep going.

Yet, though I would hate a return to that isolation, in some ways it was exactly what I needed. At the back of my mind, I had been puzzling about my origins for years, but I had always been too busy and preoccupied to really think about what it all meant. When I was younger, my life was so full of parties and travel and work and fun that I had not thought about my biological family all that often, apart from around the time of my birthday. Now that I was in my forties, and having been through a near-death experience a few years before, the questions about my origins and early childhood were on my mind more frequently, although I still had a busy life and not that much time to think about it.

For the last few years, I had avoided TV shows like *Long Lost Families* because I found myself getting upset when I saw programmes about other people meeting their biological relatives for the first time, even though I was not a hundred per cent sure that I wanted to do the same thing, and even though I knew that the TV producers carefully selected the families they chose to feature, and then edited the show to present a particular point of view that was often much more positive than the reality. Now, during lockdown, my questions came into sharp focus.

At that time, the media was full of horrifying disclosures about how the mother and baby homes had been run throughout much of the twentieth century, including the scandal of the Tuam mother and baby home which was brought to national attention by historian Catherine Corless. By that stage, we had all heard sufficient stories about Ireland's shortcomings in terms of how it cared for its most vulnerable citizens to know that, throughout our history, as a nation we failed them terribly.

But the accounts of what happened in Tuam added a whole new level of horror, because the babies who had died there – often from preventable disease and from neglect – were not even given a proper burial. In a culture that prides itself on the compassion with which it treats the bereaved and the deceased, those babies had been stacked one on top of another in disused septic tanks, like the rubbish that apparently many saw them as. The people who were being paid by the state to take care of the children in the homes literally treated those infants as if they were bodily waste. Their tiny skeletons were now so intermingled that it would take years for a forensic anthropologist to figure out which remains belonged together. This was a detail so grotesque that it was tempting to try not to believe it, but it was horribly true. Only someone with a heart of stone could have heard those stories and not felt devastated by the awfulness of it all. The evidence spoke for itself.

Hundreds of people rang radio talk shows to share their stories, or the stories of their family members. I like to listen to the radio in the car, and on one level I was curious to hear those accounts, but I often had to turn them off, as I just could not cope with what I was hearing. I had often imagined what my biological mother, Elizabeth, had gone through when she had me, but my imaginings had always been quite soft-focus, because I knew so little about the nature of institutional care at the time.

The awful stories coming out of Tuam made me feel so grateful for my own happy ending, while also angry about the horrors that so many other children in mother and baby homes endured. I wondered how many people's experiences were similar to mine; how many of us had been raised in happy family environments, making all the difference in our early lives. I reflected on how different things had been earlier in the twentieth century. Had I been born a generation sooner, I could easily have been one of the babies in Tuam, dead through neglect and cast aside.

About five years before, I had started, but then halted, an investigation into my origins. While I had always had questions, I had not felt ready to know the truth, and had reasoned that, as I have such a loving adoptive family, I did not really need to know. But as the news about the mother and baby homes continued to fill the airwaves, my desire to learn where I had come from grew and grew until I could no longer ignore it. It became a sort of hunger that I could feel all the time; a burning sensation in my stomach that I knew would only be satisfied when I had access to knowledge about my start in life.

One day, I went online and searched for information about other people who were born into the Irish mother and baby homes. I quickly discovered that there were lots of groups on Facebook and on other social media, with thousands of members who, like me, were born to single mothers in mother and baby homes, or whose custody was handed over to the state for one reason or another. Many of them, like me, had been adopted. Some were the biological mothers of children who had grown up in homes, now elderly and trying to make contact with them while there was still time to do so.

At first I just read others' stories, but gradually I started to interact with people in the forums. Many were very anxious about the road ahead. The biological mothers often asked the group members if they thought the children they had given birth to many years before would want to know them now. People who had been adopted, or who had grown up in industrial schools, had similar questions.

Others shared stories about their own experiences of meeting their biological families for the first time. Often, these stories were deeply sad, because in so many cases the longed-for bond just was not there, and these meetings could even reopen old wounds and bring a lot of feelings of hurt and anguish to the fore. Sometimes, the big reunion between a mother and her child was like throwing a hand grenade into a family, as women who were now getting on in years had to tell their other children – and sometimes their husbands too – that they had given birth to another baby, many years before.

In the forums, many people spoke very frankly about the complex emotions they had experienced on meeting their relatives after so many years. While there were certainly stories about joyful reunions, in many cases the negative emotions of anger, shame and sorrow that were stirred up by these encounters left people wondering if maybe they should not have tried to get in contact at all. Even when the reunions went relatively well, there could be heartache when people did not necessarily want the same things from one another. I remember one biological mother who was absolutely devastated because she had felt such an overwhelming sense of love for and connection to her adult daughter when they finally met that she wanted to see her all the time, whereas her daughter said that all she wanted was an occasional catch-up rather than a close relationship.

There was also a lot of heartbreak for people whose experiences with their adoptive families had not been great, or who had grown up in industrial homes. Many of them had fantasized over the years about how wonderful it would be when they finally made contact with their biological families, and in many cases the reality was a huge let-down. Sometimes the birth mothers refused to provide the information they were asked for, about the circumstances of the babies' births, the identity of the fathers, and why they had felt they had no choice but to give their children up. Sometimes the adult children met their biological families, and simply found that they had nothing in common with them at all. Sometimes they did not even like them. Sometimes they wished that they had never started to look for them.

While many people seemed to have had rich and fulfilling lives despite a difficult beginning, there were also quite a few who appeared to have been irrevocably damaged by the traumas they had experienced. There were elderly women who had spent their entire lives mourning for the babies they had given up, and adoptees whose childhoods had been blighted by their longing for a life that they would never have, and biological parents they would never know. There were people who had lived with mental illness, alcoholism and drug abuse, because they had not been able to find another way to fill the gaping holes in their lives left there by all their unanswered questions.

Reading other people's stories, and interacting with the mothers and former residents of the mother and baby homes and industrial schools, was an eye-opening experience for me. On the one hand, it reminded me once again of how blessed I have been in my life, because I have never doubted my family's love. I even felt slightly ashamed and guilty about having had such a wonderful childhood just because of my good fortune in the Penroses coming into my life when other children, who deserved happiness as much as I did, had endured terribly difficult early years. On the other hand, it made me wonder again what it would be like to make contact with my biological mother's family. Would I be one of the fortunate ones who felt an immediate connection with her biological relatives, or would meeting them be a disaster that I would regret for the rest of my life?

Despite the fact that so many people seemed to have found it very stressful and difficult meeting their biological families for the first time, I was increasingly drawn to the idea of finding mine – even though I already suspected that my mother was dead. I wondered what it would be like for them if I managed to trace them. Would Elizabeth's siblings, if they were still alive, be happy to see me? Was my birth a secret that they also had to keep hidden from the world, or had they thought about me occasionally over the years and wondered how I was doing? Was there, out there somewhere, a family of sisters and brothers, children of the same mother, who look a little like me and who would like to welcome me into their family circle? Or would I just be an unwelcome reminder of the fact that, a long time ago, their mother did something that was then considered shameful, and ended up having me as a result? Would they look at my face and, instead of searching my features for a resemblance, feel ashamed of their mother for having had a relationship with a Black man? Would my very existence be a source of embarrassment to them?

I had often wondered about the woman who gave birth to me – about Elizabeth – but as more details about the mother and baby homes emerged, I started to think about her in a more focused way. I wondered if Elizabeth had been mistreated during her pregnancy; if she had been coerced into giving me up; if she had been made to feel humiliated, punished and ashamed for having become pregnant with me. If she had been told, or had come to believe, that my scoliosis was the result of God's judgement on her for having sex before marriage. If the very fact of my existence had tortured her all her life, a reminder of the dark days she had spent in a punitive mother and baby home. Or if she was one of the more fortunate ones, grateful for help at a difficult time, and ready to move on with the rest of her life as soon as she was out of hot water.

I wondered about other things too. Even though I was very delicate when I was small and was prone to chest infections and other health issues, I never caught any of the infectious diseases that were doing the rounds in our school or neighbourhood. My parents did not have detailed medical records from my time in St Patrick's, but Mam was told that I had every vaccination going, and history has revealed that the children in Irish institutions were often used in vaccine and other medical trials, as they had no parents to raise objections. I know that I was in St Patrick's when vaccine trials were carried out on the children there, and I am sure that the home was paid well for providing the children for the trial, but I have not been able to find confirmation of my having been included. I have checked the records, and even contacted GlaxoSmithKline, the pharmaceutical company that did the research. I guess I will never know for sure.

The vast majority of the people in the forums were from

Irish backgrounds – or were assumed to be, because they were white, and looked like everyone else. Only a tiny minority of the people I met were from mixed backgrounds like mine. Then, in one of the forums for people who had spent time at St Patrick's, I made contact with a man called Conrad Bryan, who had also been born there; most of the people in the group introduced themselves by saying when they had been there, and how long they had stayed. Many of us overlapped, but Conrad was a bit older, and had spent time at the home before I was born. He and I started to chat online, and when I told him that I live near Drogheda now, he said that he had actually grown up in an industrial school in the town and that he knew it well.

'I live in London now,' he said, 'but I'll be over for a visit one of these days. Maybe we could meet for a coffee.'

Some months afterwards, Conrad and I were sitting opposite one another in a coffee shop in Drogheda.

'I can hardly believe this,' I said. 'It doesn't seem real.'

Finally, I was meeting someone in person who looked and sounded quite like me: Black and Irish at once. I immediately warmed to Conrad and, although this was the first time we had met face to face, I felt that we were already friends.

We ordered our coffees and started to chat. Conrad was warm, open and friendly, and he quickly shared the basic details of his life story with me. I learned that, like me, his biological mother was white and his father was Black. Like me, too, he had been a ward of state for his whole childhood. That was where our similarities ended, because instead of growing up with a loving family, as I did, Conrad grew up in an industrial school, and while he was fostered out with a local family, who were very kind to him, for some of his childhood, overall he had a much more difficult time than me. Yet, while many people who have grown up in care are left with such profound psychological scars that they struggle to build their careers and a successful home life, Conrad has done extremely well professionally, and has an excellent job as an accountant, and a fantastic wife and family. He is a very impressive person, and I have huge admiration for him.

Conrad asked me if I would be interested in making a submission to the Mother and Baby Homes Commission, which was interviewing people who had passed through the system with a view to writing up a report on it. I told him that I would be very keen to do so, and he promised to pass on my details. He also told me that he was involved with an organization called AMRI, the Association of Mixed Race in Ireland, which he and others had set up in 2016 to provide a point of contact and support for Irish people of mixed racial heritage, whether or not they had grown up in state care. The aim of the association was to seek justice from the state for the racism its members experienced as children in Irish institutions. The racial abuses and discrimination were detailed in the 2009 Ryan Report on abuses in Irish industrial schools, but they had not been acknowledged and recognized by the state in its redress scheme at that time. As AMRI's scope grew, Conrad was joined by others.

'There are loads of us out there,' Conrad said with a smile. 'But because we've never spoken out with one voice, a lot of people don't realize it. There have always been more Black and mixed-race people in Ireland than most people know. We think it's time we were heard.'

While I had never been lonely, exactly, because I have always been surrounded by my family and friends, I had often felt alone in my Blackness. Throughout most of my life, I had been the only Black person at every family party, in every classroom, every gathering of friends. And dearly as I love my family and friends, they will never know what it feels like to walk into a room and be the single Black person there. The only time I had ever not felt keenly aware of my minority status had been in places like Heathrow Airport or downtown London or New York, where there are so many different types of people. I absolutely loved the thought of meeting and getting to know other Irish people like Conrad and me; the thought of being just one of many in a room who had a similar appearance, and similar experiences of Irishness. Conrad asked me if I would like to get involved.

'God, yeah,' I said. 'Where do I sign up?'

Shortly after meeting Conrad, by which stage Ireland had closed up again because of the Covid pandemic, he used Zoom to introduce me to some of the other founding members, including Jude Hughes, who has also been involved with AMRI from the start, and Dr Phil Mullen, who is Professor of Black Studies at Trinity College Dublin. Jude is a generation older again, and he grew up in the mother-and-baby-home and industrial-school complex at a time when the children in state care were often treated extremely badly. Today, he is a highly skilled tailor, a veteran campaigner for human rights and against racism, and a wonderful person. Together with the other members of the organization, Conrad, Jude and Phil work tirelessly to support mixed-race Irish people and to raise awareness about us. They were all very kind and welcoming to me. I was deeply impressed by their dedication and passion and very grateful to have the opportunity to get to know them and talk to people with whom I have so much in common.

At around this time, I wrote the article that was published on the Black and Irish social media feed; the article that kick-started a big change in my life and that I mentioned in the prologue. I hoped that, by putting my story out there, maybe I had been able to reach some people who rarely thought about the things I had discussed. I had been feeling quite alone, quite different, since starting to think about finding out more about my biological family, but now I realized that I was not alone at all; rather, there were countless people in my situation, and countless more who were, or wanted to be, there for us.

Not long after the article was featured, Ailish, the producer from *The Ryan Tubridy Show* on RTÉ Radio One, contacted me, asking if I would be prepared to do an interview. (I found out that Dad had sent her a copy of the piece.) I was petrified at the thought of it, but I said yes, and we arranged to have a meeting by phone.

'It'll be no bother to you,' Ailish said reassuringly. 'I can tell after talking to you for a few minutes that you'll be absolutely grand. You're not shy and you'll be well able to speak for yourself. I have no concerns whatsoever. You come across really well, and we'd love to have you on board for the show.'

Although the Covid pandemic was still a problem, we agreed that I would come in to the RTÉ studios in Donnybrook to do the radio interview, as they were confident that they had good systems in place to avoid the spread of the virus there. The numbers of infected people had fallen a lot over the summer, and I felt that I would be much more relaxed if I could be interviewed in person rather than on Zoom or over the phone.

In August 2020, I did the interview with Ryan. Right up until the day before, it had not really sunk in that I was doing it. That night, as I was getting ready for bed, I started to have second thoughts, wondering if maybe I should ring and leave a voicemail message saying that I was sorry, but I was not going to be able to make it after all. I could hardly believe that I had actually agreed to go on national radio and lay my life story out for all to listen to and comment on.

Then I gave myself a talking-to: I had made a commitment, I told myself sternly, and it was too late to chicken out now. My story was an important one; look at how many of the people who had read it online had responded, how many had sent me kind messages saying that I had helped them to understand what it is like being Black and Irish. In the end, I was too proud to cancel. I had made a promise, and I was determined to see it through.

I woke at three in the morning feeling absolutely awful. My stomach was churning as it always does when I am anxious – or even when I am excited and looking forward to something – my heart was pounding, and there was no way I was going to be able to get back to sleep. I got up, had a shower, and forced myself to eat some breakfast. Fortunately, I had arranged to go to the RTÉ studios with my parents, because I was shaking all the way there, and I do not think I could have driven safely if I had gone on my own.

When we got to the studios, Dad parked and he and Mam accompanied me into the building, where we met Ailish. She was so friendly and relaxed, she helped me feel at home as she told us where we could wait until it was my turn, and then brought me to the studio downstairs when it was time.

Ryan and I had a couple of minutes together during a commercial break. He was kind and very approachable, and he seemed genuinely interested in my story. Although I had been nervous going into the studios, he put me at my ease straight away.

'There's no need to be anxious,' he said firmly. 'If I can see that you need help, I'll jump in with a question, so you can feel sure that there won't be any awkward silences. You feel free to tell your story whatever way you want to.'

All at once, the commercial break was over and I was on. As Ryan turned to me, a wave of calmness came over me and, just like that, I was able to talk. Suddenly I found myself telling my story, including parts of it that I had never shared with even my dearest friends, to the entire country.

Ryan cut to a commercial break and gave me a big smile.

'Your story is really amazing,' he said. 'It'd be great to see it reaching a wider audience, because I know we've only touched on it a little bit today. There's only so much you can do in one short radio interview.'

During the commercial break, people were contacting RTÉ and leaving comments and questions. Some of them were old neighbours and friends, getting in touch to wish me well. Others were members of the public whom I had never met, commenting on my story and saying that it had given them new insights into what it was like being Black and Irish, or just saying how happy they were that I had found a wonderful family and had a good life.

By the time the interview was over, I had been talking for twenty-five minutes, but it had felt like a moment. I said goodbye to Ryan and went back out to where my parents were sitting. They both had huge grins on their faces as I approached.

'You did so well!' said Dad. 'You were amazing!'

'Not that we ever doubted you,' Mam added hastily.

As I was leaving the studios, the woman on the reception desk called after me.

'Someone rang in for you,' she said. 'She left a message.'

For a wild moment I thought that maybe I had been wrong about my biological mother, that perhaps she was still alive and reaching out to me. I was almost relieved when it turned out to be someone else.

And that was how Catherine found me. She had worked in St Patrick's, and when she heard me speak and heard my name, she realized that I was the baby girl whom she had cared for many years before. She had left her contact details and said that if I would like to get in touch with her, she would be delighted to hear from me.

My phone was hopping in my hand all the way home as friends and relatives rang me to say that they had heard the interview. My friend Ruth, whom I had met at work in the cosmetics store several years earlier, and who has remained very close ever since, was nearly hysterical and I was almost worried there was something wrong with her.

'I can't understand you!' I said, and in an aside to Mam: 'Mam, there's something wrong with Ruth.'

'I never knew a quarter of the stuff you said about your life,' Ruth eventually was able to say. 'You never talk about any of that.'

Ruth was right. I love my life, and the fantastic relationships I have with my family and friends. I always like to live in the moment and focus on the positive.

When I got home, I scrolled through the social media feed of *The Ryan Tubridy Show* to see what people were saying about the interview. Most of the comments were kind and supportive, but one or two cast scorn on the very idea of my describing myself as Black, saying that, as a mixed-race person, I had no right to the label. That hurt a little because, like all mixed-race people, I know that when people see me, they see a Black person – and that for those who are racist, the details of where a dark-skinned person's genes come from are irrelevant, because all they see, and all they care about, is difference.

'Are you going to ring the lady?' Dad asked. 'The one who minded you when you were little? You should ring her straight away!'

'Oh God no,' I said. 'I'm in no fit state. Not yet.'

I could feel my heart rate was still elevated as I gradually came down from the adrenaline high that had been keeping me going since the night before.

That evening, back in my own apartment, I texted the number the receptionist had given me and introduced myself. Minutes later, Catherine rang me back. We spoke for over an hour. I had been a little nervous about how it would go, but we seemed to have an instant connection, and the conversation flowed as though she was somebody I had known all my life. Perhaps it was an illusion, or even a little bit of wishful thinking, but her kind voice sounded familiar to me.

Catherine told me that, although her time at the mother and baby home had been relatively brief, she had often wondered about the children whom she had taken care of, and especially about me, as we had shared a special bond. She had spent some years nursing in England, and had returned to Ireland, married, and now had three grown-up daughters of her own, but she had never forgotten me, and she had always kept an eye out when she was in Dublin, just in case she recognized me.

Catherine and I agreed that, when the lockdown was over and the time was right, we would meet up and she would tell me everything she could about my early years.

Two months after that, in October 2020, my caseworker from Tusla, the Irish child and family agency, rang and asked if I was still interested in learning about my biological family. A few months before, the records of St Patrick's and a number of other mother and baby homes had been transferred to Tusla. This was a controversial step, because the government had also announced that it planned to seal the records for thirty years, and many of the people who had been born in, and who had grown up in, institutions were very angry that their stories were not going to be brought to light. Be that as it may, I had been assigned a caseworker and now she was reaching out.

My caseworker arranged for the two of us to have a Zoom meeting as we could not meet in person during lockdown. Again, I was a little nervous, but when it actually happened, she helped me relax quite quickly, smiling at me on my computer screen and telling me not to worry, that she would be there every step of the way. We talked about what the process would be like, what my expectations were, and what I could reasonably expect to happen. She warned me that finding out information about an adoptee's biological family could be very slow and very frustrating, and that I should not get my hopes up. I told her that I understood, and assured her that my expectations were realistic. I was relieved to find that she and I had a good rapport, as I had been afraid that it would all be very difficult, especially as we could not even meet in person.

While all of this was going on, the commission into the mother and baby homes in Ireland – yet another exercise in revisiting the country's long history of the shameful treatment of unmarried women and girls and their babies and children – was winding up after five years of investigations. While there was still time for me to give my testimony, I was invited to attend an interview and tell my story.

I told the commission as much as I could, which was not very much. The two women in front of me were polite, friendly and informal, and the interview was essentially a chat about my experience of having been adopted. Because my few memories of St Patrick's are so vague, it was relatively short, just an hour or so. I left the meeting feeling quite positive, and hopeful that the commission would help to bring peace to the many people who had passed through the mother and baby homes. I was also optimistic that we would all be given access to information about our birth, our biological relatives and our medical history, for so long denied us. After all these years, I naively felt – as I still do – that we all deserved it.

In late November 2020, Conrad got in touch. A BBC reporter had heard about the Association for Mixed Race in Ireland, and she wanted to do an extended article about the work the organization did.

'She wants to feature some of our stories,' Conrad explained. 'Would you be willing to share yours?'

I felt that, as my story was already public, there was no reason why not, and I agreed. Shortly after that, I did the interview with the journalist, a lovely woman called Deirdre Finnerty. I could tell very quickly that Deirdre was genuinely interested in me, my story and AMRI's work. As the piece needed to be illustrated, she arranged for a photographer called Charles McQuillan to come and take my picture. I absolutely hate having my picture taken – yes, I know that everyone does, but I think that, for me, dealing with my feelings about my scoliosis in that situation adds a little extra stress – and felt a little intimidated when I googled Charles and found out that he is an award-winning photographer. When I met him, however, he put me at ease straight away and I could tell that he was not just doing a job, but was interested in the article and my contribution to it. The resulting photographs, which he took in my apartment, captured me well.

I knew, when Charles left, that the story was out of my hands now. I wondered, briefly, if I had done the right thing in letting Deirdre interview me. The thought of all those people reading about me and staring at my features on their computer or mobile phone screens made me feel very exposed. Then I told myself that it would be grand. If people found the story interesting and felt inspired to learn more about those who are Black and Irish, like me, that would be great. If they hated it, so what? That was not my problem.

When the final piece, entitled *The Hidden Story of African-Irish Children*, was published on the BBC website, it got countless hits; over a million within two days. Of course, as soon as I knew it was up, I went straight to take a look. It was really weird seeing my own familiar face on the screen under the BBC logo, but I was able to be objective enough to realize how important the photographs of me and Jude and Conrad were. Without our faces to illustrate the story, it was just data. The images showed the people behind statistics that are otherwise hard to understand as people's actual lives.

Our stories really resonated with the readers, and most of the responses were absolutely amazing. Once again, my phone was buzzing with people getting in touch to tell me that they had seen my story and they wanted to congratulate me for going public with it. Deirdre emailed me excitedly to say that the piece had really taken off and that huge numbers of people all over the world were not just reading it but forwarding it to their friends and sharing it on their social media feeds.

I had told just a handful of people about the interview, so a lot of my friends only found out about it when they logged on to the BBC website to read the news and saw my face looking back at them, or when I reposted it to publicize the story. Some of the people who contacted me were Africans who had seen the article and wanted to help me locate my relatives. Unfortunately, as I know so little, it is impossible to know where to start.

A few days later, on 9th December 2020, my caseworker confirmed what I already knew, deep down: my biological mother was dead, and I was never going to get to meet her because it was too late. Elizabeth had passed away some years before. She had spent all her life in Dublin, and was buried somewhere in the city, but my caseworker did not have permission to tell me where she was.

For a moment, I stared at the computer screen, digesting the news.

'OK,' I said. 'Yeah.'

'Are you all right?' she asked.

'I am, yeah,' I said.

Then I burst into tears.

I honestly believe that we all have some sort of instinctive connection with our blood relations, with our ancestors, because on some level I had already been sure that my biological mother was dead. Still, it was a shock to hear it being confirmed aloud. I sat and cried in front of the computer while my poor caseworker tried to comfort me as best she could, under circumstances that were very far from ideal; I could see her anxious, pixelated face getting close to the screen as she said gentle words to me, and I knew that she wanted to do more for me than a Zoom call allowed for. She was so kind, and I would like to put it on record that, while Tusla often get a very bad rap in the Irish media, they have some lovely people working for them. My caseworker was unfailingly considerate, and I could tell that she really cared about me and my well-being and that she was doing her best to protect me. While I know that not everybody has been treated with such kindness by the Irish state authorities, in the rush to condemn, I feel that the media has sometimes overlooked the constraints that Tusla are under.

'It's weird,' my caseworker said, when I had calmed down a little, 'the way you sort of already knew she wasn't alive.'

'Yeah,' I said. 'I didn't think I'd get this upset. My adoptive parents have always been my mam and dad and I had such a happy childhood.'

After we'd finished our conversation, I closed my laptop and sat alone in my apartment for a little while, thinking about things. I wished that I could go to my parents' house to tell them about it all, but after the relative openness of the summer, the return of high Covid numbers meant that we were back in lockdown and all staying away from each other again, for fear of infection.

When I felt ready, I rang Mam and told her everything. She had been unaware that I had started the process of searching for my biological family, and she listened patiently as I blurted it all out, ending with the news that my case-worker had just told me that the woman who had given birth to me was dead.

'Ah, love,' said Mam. She did not need to say any more than that.

I burst into tears again. I still did not really know why I was crying, why I was so upset. But I was. Mam spoke to me softly, and said that she would tell Dad everything I had just told her, as he would want to know, and there was no reason for me to go through this journey on my own. After talking to Mam, I rang Ciara to keep her in the picture.

The next day, my caseworker sent me a text to remind me that she was only a phone call away, and that she was always there if I needed someone to talk to. I imagined that the situation must be quite frustrating for her, having access to more information about me than she was at liberty to divulge. She knew that I was full of questions, and that she had the answers to many of them, but the law simply prevented her from sharing them with me.

Since I did the interview, it seems that Ireland is still determined to hold on to its secrets. The Mother and Baby Homes Commission's report, which had been submitted to the Minister for Children, Equality, Disability, Integration and Youth on 30th October 2020, was published in January 2021 and Micheál Martin, the Taoiseach at the time, apologized to the mothers – the survivors – and their children for having been treated so inhumanely by the state. The interviewees were not routinely sent copies of the report, but rather had to request one several weeks after its publication, so a lot of other people read it before we did, which I found very insulting. As one of the contributors, I ordered a copy and it was duly delivered to me, hundreds of pages in an enormous box. Reading through it, I could see that while some of the horrors were discussed – my heart broke when I read about the women who were forced to care for other mothers' babies when their own had just been taken from them – many issues were glossed over and left out. Above all, the report failed to discuss or attempt to justify the fact that, for many years, the forced separation of mothers and their children was effectively state policy. It is easy to blame the nuns who generally ran the homes, but they cannot shoulder all the guilt, because successive governments over the years were only too happy to abdicate all responsibility to them.

Like me, many of the former residents of mother and baby homes are not happy with how the research that led to the report was carried out, or with some of the conclusions it reached. While many testified about forced adoption and abuse, the commission concluded that there was a lack of evidence for this, and many of those who gave testimony reported that the things they said were subsequently misrepresented, or that forged material was included in their files. When I think of the many women who were mistreated in the system, forced or coerced to give away their babies, I feel absolutely enraged. We cannot undo the past, but the least we can do now is acknowledge the pain and suffering that resulted from what was once official state policy. The commission also falls short in failing to recognize the racism and discrimination towards children with disabilities that prevailed throughout the system.

While I think a lot of people participated in the commission's research in the desire that their words would bring some closure to a very unhappy chapter in Ireland's history, most of us are very disillusioned now. Official Ireland has lost interest and moved on, and we, the mothers and children of the homes, are still here, with nothing but questions. I am sure that the authorities hope that, by dragging their investigations out for as long as they can, eventually all of the survivors will give up and die off. I do not like to be pessimistic, but I do believe that most of our questions are fated to remain unanswered.

12. I'm Black; I'm Irish; I'm Me

When I started writing this book, I felt very positive about doing it, about my life so far, and about the future. While I was a little nervous about the process, I was also proud about starting to tell my story, and sharing it with the world.

I also started having nightmares for the first time in many years. I found myself waking up in the middle of the night with my heart racing, and my head buzzing with images, feelings and thoughts. I dreamt about babies and children being left alone in great big rooms, about little girls in hospital, about reaching my arms up towards someone, hoping to be touched, and no touch coming. My painful memories, which I have striven hard to keep below the surface, were finally working their way out, and it hurt.

At first I was worried about what the nightmares meant. I even wondered if I was doing myself harm and should stop thinking about the past. After all, I have been future-focused all my life and, generally speaking, that has worked very well for me. But as I continued to write and to dredge through my memories, I accepted that, at last, I had no choice but to confront and process my experiences. While it continued to be agonizing and difficult at times to expose to the light thoughts and worries that I usually keep buried, I could also see that it was good for me, much like the awful physiotherapy that I have had to endure every time I have had a surgical intervention; it hurts, but it is for the best.

Ireland's second big lockdown, the winter of 2020–21,

was the perfect time for me to go through this process. I spent many evenings with just my little dog Mia for company, and I had all the time in the world to think about where I come from, about the people who gave me my distinctive looks. About the families that never got to see me growing up. Although that winter was difficult for me, as it was for everyone, in some ways I had a positive experience of lockdown because I took the time I needed to think long and hard about who I am, where I come from, and what I would like my legacy to be.

Of course, I thought about my biological parents when I was growing up, but I was also very secure in my adoptive family. Now, I wondered more and more if my biological parents had thought about me often, all the years of my childhood. Had they hoped that I was happy? Worried that things might be tough sometimes because I did not look like the other little girls? Hoped that the doctors might be able to fix my back and make me stand straighter? Wondered about what might have been, if things had been different, and they had been able to bring me up themselves?

In April 2021, after I started working on this book, a woman called Marie-Claire Logue got in touch with me. Twenty years before, her father, Paddy Logue, had compiled a book of essays by a range of people discussing what being Irish meant to them, and published it under the title *Being Irish*. Marie-Claire wanted to publish an updated version that reflected all the changes that had taken place in Ireland since then, and in particular how much more multicultural Ireland has become. She asked me if I could contribute a piece, and I agreed that I would.

Once again, I found myself having to try to look objectively at my life and my experiences, and to explain to other people what it feels like being Black and Irish at the same time. As I hit the 'send' button, I was anxious that I had not written my thoughts down sufficiently clearly and that Marie-Claire might have to tell me that my piece was not good enough for her book. Instead, she sent me a lovely email saying that it would be a very valuable addition. This felt like confirmation that I should continue writing my book, because people would care about my story and would want to know more.

Obviously, as the only Black member of my family, I have always been keenly aware of my appearance and of the fact that I am a mixed-race Irish woman. The evidence for that stares me in the face every time I stand in front of the mirror to do my make-up or brush my hair. Even though I could never forget that I had been adopted, because I stand out so much in our family photographs, I have always known that my parents and my sister, and my many aunts, uncles and cousins, gave me all the love and sense of self I needed. For years, I had told myself that that was enough. Who cared what colour my skin was?

The reality, of course, is that a lot of people *do* care what colour my skin is, and that they judge me for it. Because I know at first hand how difficult it can be belonging to a minority, I have always been an advocate among my friends and at work for racial equality and for treating everyone equally, regardless of what they look like and where they come from. But now I started to think about race and racism in a deeper way, delving into what I already knew from reading about political movements at various points in history, like the Black Panthers and the anti-apartheid movement in South Africa, and into what I had learned from prominent Black writers such as Maya Angelou.

I thought more deeply about my Irishness too; about my strong sense of belonging here, about my love of Dublin, where I grew up, and about the fact that, because of how I look, some people struggle to accept me as a 'real' Irish person. I found myself having to confront a series of questions that could be very difficult to unpick. What does it mean, *really*, to be Black and Irish? Am I less Irish because I am Black? Less Black because I am Irish? Am I Irish in a different way, for example, to a child growing up here with parents who are white, but from other cultures? I know that there are plenty of people who would answer 'yes' to all of those questions.

The roots and causes of racism are complicated and can be difficult to understand – and, I have to admit, I was still figuring a lot of this out. Perhaps it was partly because I was getting older too – in my mid-forties, now – but I realized that I did want to know more about race and racism in general and about my cultural background in particular, and also to live my identity as a Black Irish woman in a more decisive way. To take charge of my identity and embrace the things that make me different to, as well as the things that make me the same as, the other people in my life. Although I do struggle with body consciousness, for obvious reasons, I have always been proud of who I am and what I look like, but I wanted to tease out this feeling, to understand it, and to find a way to communicate it.

While I had experienced isolated incidents of racism throughout my teens and early twenties, when most people asked where I was really from they did not mean to be intrusive or unkind, although they were often unintentionally rude, and could be very invasive, like when strangers wanted to touch my hair and feel its texture between their fingers, or compared the colour of my skin to types of food – coffee, chocolate, caramel. Sometimes, while pointing out that I am not white, they also stressed their refusal to see me as Black: 'You're not really Black, though. You're more of a *beige* . . .' I think some of them actually thought that, by sharing their view that I am not a 'real' Black person, they were giving me a compliment.

Most of these people were genuinely curious about my unusual appearance and did not realize that their words could be interpreted as hurtful. They would have been absolutely horrified if someone had told them that they were being racist by singling me out for special attention because of my appearance. They would have been very taken aback if I had started talking to them the way they talked to me, comparing their skin to yoghurt, mayonnaise or raspberry ripple ice cream, to point out how ridiculous they were being. The behaviour of that girl on Grafton Street who had berated me after a night out on the town, just because she did not like the way I looked, had been so upsetting partly because it was so unusual. But these people, whether they knew it or not, were being racist too – even if they did not mean to be.

For a long time, there were so few Black people in Ireland that I often felt very alone in having these sorts of experience. Black people in Ireland – or at least the ones I was aware of – were mostly famous for one thing or another, like Phil Lynott and Paul McGrath. These national heroes obviously were accepted by the general public because they had achieved so much and people were proud to claim them as Irish because they represented the country so well. But most Black people in Ireland are not famous and never will be – and you should not have to be famous to be accepted.

As Ireland became more multicultural, I started hearing

about other people experiencing similar things, and anonymous – and sometimes not anonymous – commentators on the Internet were making all sorts of racist slurs about anyone who did not look the way they thought an Irish person should. The negative side of Ireland's increasing multiculturalism was the parallel growth in aggressive racism and a growing boldness in expressing racist sentiments that, before, people might have thought, but had been too ashamed to say out loud. The fact that everyone was online now made it awfully easy to say those terrible words.

Also striking was the fact that people felt the need to stress the colour of someone's skin if that person had annoyed or disappointed them in some way, or indeed even if they had done anything at all of note, even something seen positively: 'the Black taxi-driver's cab was dirty'; 'the Black nurse was very rude'; 'that nice Black man carried my shopping out to the car for me'. I could not help noticing that they did not feel the need to stress the whiteness of people who attracted their attention. Nobody ever remarked that they had had poor service from the white girl in the supermarket. I knew, if I ever encountered a person like this as I went about my work, that my colour, my difference, would suddenly become an issue for them if they perceived me as rude or my work as anything less than excellent.

I was very glad, as I continued to think more and more about all of these issues, for having met Conrad and Jude and the rest of the AMRI community. They are incredible people. In a quiet, unobtrusive way, they offer huge support to each of the members, especially in terms of providing us all with a unified voice. In the case of those who grew up in state care, or who were adopted as children, they give them information and help with searching for their biological parents from other countries and cultures, and with practical advice on finding housing and work. I was honoured to be asked to join them in the work that they do. I am a proud member of AMRI.

As the lockdown was still in force, and as quite a few of the members were based in the UK, my first AMRI meetings were held on Zoom. It was strange, but wonderful, sitting on the sofa in my apartment, looking at the screen as one person after another entered the meeting and said hello. Witnessing the array of faces of mixed-race people on my computer and hearing everyone speak was extraordinary. It was the first time ever I'd taken part in a meeting with loads of people who look like me. There, I was just one of many, and while each of us had a unique experience of being Irish and mixed-race, we shared in common our Irish culture and mixed-race heritage. While I had never met most of them in person, and had no reason to assume that any of us would have much in common other than our skin colour, I felt a profound sense of connection, even of love, for the strangers on my screen.

Conrad and I continued to talk, and he started helping me to find out more about my father. I was able to tell him that a number of Zambians came and stayed at the army barracks in Kildare in the 1970s, and Conrad learned that most of them have since passed away. That was a blow, but as I continued on my journey of self-discovery, I understood that modern technology might have given me some of the tools I needed to find out more about where I come from. For a long time I had been very frustrated about not being able to learn more about my biological father. People could hide files and records, I realized, but nobody owns my genetic material other than me. I hoped that my genes would provide the answers to the questions I have lived with my whole life.

I know that people have a lot of very well-founded concerns about privacy when it comes to the various companies that offer gene-testing services, but I felt I was prepared to take the risk if I had the chance to find out more about myself. When one of the staff at work, Dr Sheila, offered me a MyHeritage kit following our conversations about my family background, I took it from her and looked at the box, my heart beating fast. Was I ready, I wondered, to deal with whatever I might find out? I contacted Conrad and we talked about what might happen.

'Just be prepared,' he said. 'Don't be surprised if it turns out that your family comes from somewhere different to what you've been told.'

Because I was not sure what to expect, I tried not to get too excited about it. I discussed the test with my family, and said that I had no idea what I might find out, if anything. They agreed that it was a good idea, and we all hoped that the results might help me to start understanding my background a little more. I had to fill a test tube with saliva, seal it shut and send it off to the company. A few weeks later, the results came back. They showed that my ethnic background is even more complex than I thought, as I share genes with people from all over the world, including Scandinavia and Wales. I also have genes that are common in Nigeria, and there were many Nigerians and people of Nigerian origin among the thousands of distant relatives who have also signed up to the system. I felt a little deflated by the results, as they provided no meaningful answers. I do hope that if I can get more information from Tusla, or if a closer genetic relative signs up to MyHeritage, I might learn more. I suppose that time will tell.

Perhaps because I was fostered as a small child, I have always been fascinated by genetics and inheritance. I love spotting family likenesses when my family and I look back over old photographs, or when a new baby cousin is born and we pass the little bundle around and try to figure out who they look like. The fact that I have never been able to see a resemblance in myself to any family member is a source of sorrow. I don't know who I resemble, because I have never met any biological relatives of mine. There may be a Dublin family out there to whom I bear a strong likeness – and I know that by naming my biological mother in this book I am opening up the possibility that they will want to contact me – but, for now, all I have is my own face in the mirror and a lot of questions.

I have no proof that there is anything in my family history to connect me directly with the horror story of slavery in America and the Caribbean. On the one hand, I have been given no reason to believe that I am descended from people who were bought and sold in the Atlantic slave trade, as most African Americans are, although there is no way of knowing for sure. On the other hand, because – particularly in the West – the films we see, the books we read and the media we consume are so dominated by the American experience, the history of the enslavement of Black people by white people casts its long shadow, even on Black people like me, growing up elsewhere with no direct ancestral involvement at all.

On some level, the white people involved in slavery – who included plenty of Irish immigrants to the United States, and even Irish people in Ireland, where some kept slaves in the seventeenth century – must have known that what they were doing was very wrong. They went to huge lengths to justify it to themselves, such as baptizing slaves in their holding pens before they were loaded on to ships heading to America, and looking to age-old Bible stories in an attempt to confirm what they chose to see as Black inferiority. And whether we like to admit it or not here in Ireland, this sordid history does play a role in Irish racism. How could it not? We have all grown up in a society completely steeped in American cultural influences.

Another factor in Irish racism is the way in which Black people, and in particular Black African people, have traditionally been represented by charities, missionaries and other philanthropic organizations. This is all much more difficult to tease out and criticize, because obviously a lot of those organizations, and the thousands of people who have worked for them, have also done wonderful things to help those who needed it and, in general, their intentions have been very good. But in their efforts to raise essential funds for facilities like schools, hospitals and maternity units, they have often portrayed Black people in Africa – and by extension Black people everywhere – as passive, hapless, helpless victims who can never achieve their potential without a handout from some benevolent whites. I know that when I was growing up the Trócaire box did very little to challenge the view of Black people as, almost by definition, poor, pathetic and unable to progress without help and guidance from white people in the West. This, too, has certainly had a negative impact on the way Black people have historically been seen in Ireland – from state-funded organizations denying Black biological fathers any agency in their children's lives, to the blithe assumption that all Black people outside Africa are, in every way, 'better off'. This is an assumption that can prevent an exploration of what racism really is, and how badly it can damage people as individuals and society as a whole; it lets Western cultures off the hook for the various ways in which racism is experienced within them.

Because all the negative ways in which Black people have often been seen have fed into how I have been seen by Irish racists, I believe that I have every right to claim and live my Blackness. In asserting a Black identity, I am absolutely not rejecting my legacy from my biological mother, a white Irish woman, because – even though we have never really met, and now never will – I feel a lot of love towards Elizabeth. Nor am I rejecting all that my adoptive parents have given me – a wonderful childhood, unconditional love and support, and an amazing foundation on which to build my adult life. Nor again am I rejecting my Irishness, because I am very Irish, and I am happy and proud to be from our rainy green island.

Instead, I am simply refusing to reject the other side of my heritage, and I am accepting that, in all sorts of ways, when people see me they see a Black woman who evokes whatever they feel and think about the Black people they encounter, whether in person or in the media. I love using emojis in my emails and text messages, and was pleased and excited when emojis with different skin colours were made available so that I can choose symbols that represent me and that give me a way to make a little statement about who I am every time I use my email or WhatsApp. For the first time in many years, I have started thinking about going back to my natural Afro hairstyle. While I love having long, straight hair that I can wear in a ponytail or flick over my shoulder, I also regret, and feel a little guilty about, not embracing my natural curls with pride.

Although I have travelled quite widely, including to

countries with large Black minority populations, I have never been to Africa. For years, going there has been one of my greatest dreams. I always loved watching documentaries about Africa and Africans, and I long to have the experience of being in an African country in which white people are a small minority. I always thought that, when I knew a little more about my biological father, I would go to the place where he came from. I imagined placing my feet where he walked, smelling the things he smelled, and tasting the dishes that he grew up eating. However, the more I try to find out about him, the less certain I am of even the few details I have been told. The reality is that I do not know for sure if he was from Zambia at all and, as Africa is enormous, he could be from almost any country in it – or even, possibly, from the Caribbean. If I plan a trip to Africa, when I get there I could still be many thousands of miles away from any place he ever went.

I have started to accept that I might never learn about my father, might never know who he was and where he came from. This is painful, but it also makes it easier for me to think about going to Africa for the first time, because I am finally beginning to feel able to set aside my longing to know the specifics about my origins. When this book finally hits the shelves, I might feel ready to buy a ticket to a destination in Africa and fulfil my dream.

On the other hand, I am acutely aware that it is more than likely that at least some of my biological relatives from Dublin still live in Dublin or Ireland, and I realize that, in writing this book, I am putting my story out there and inviting them to get to know me. One of them may read these pages and figure out who I am. I imagine that he or she might shut the book then to look closely at my photograph on the cover.

They will touch it with their fingers and examine my face for a resemblance to their own. And then, although they have not asked for it, they will have to wonder whether or not they want to know me.

I understand that I am asking a lot, and that seeing me in person for the first time might stir up a lot of very difficult emotions and feelings that are hard to process. But, while I imagine that our first encounter would probably be difficult for me too, I want to say that I would welcome the contact and the opportunity to get to know them as much or as little as they feel comfortable with – and that, if they do not want to meet me, that is OK too. Whatever happens, I will always wish them the best.

My relationship with disability is much more complicated than my relationship with my mixed heritage. Although I have experienced racism, I love my black hair and eyes and my dark skin, and I always have. The only thing I regret about my skin is that it is not darker and, unlike some people, I have never wanted to be white. Having a disability is different, because of course, despite the fact that I have a wonderful life in more ways than I can count, if I could choose, I would choose not to be disabled at all.

For years, I actually rejected the idea of myself as disabled, because – thanks in large part to the positive way in which I was reared – I never let my scoliosis stop me from doing anything. I have been very fortunate in my various places of work, as unlike many people who live with disability, I have never been discriminated against at all because of my physical limitations. As Mam and Dad always said, I might not be able to do everything in exactly the same way as everyone else, but I can generally figure out another way.

Looking at myself as objectively as I can, I can see that my positive nature and tendency to reject labels is my way of coping with a reality that can actually be quite difficult at times; more difficult than I am generally able to admit. I am positive all the time because I have to be. How would I have got through all of that surgery, physiotherapy and pain without being positive? How would I have recovered from respiratory failure if I had lain there and given up? I love the fact that I am a sunny-side-up person, but I would not say that it was a choice, because there really is no alternative. I hate to admit it, but the fact that I was born with such severe scoliosis, and the various medical misadventures I have had throughout my life, has played a big role in every single decision I have taken, from having to think about a route that I can manage on my own every time I arrange to meet a friend for lunch, to the big things, like having to confront the reality that getting older may be tougher for me, physically, than it is for others, because my body has already been through so much, and has to work harder than other people's just to get through a normal day. While I have always worked, not every type of work is available to me. While I have always had a very active social life, I often have to modify the plans I make with my friends, because I cannot always keep up with them. While people often tell me that I have a very attractive face, and that they love the way I dress, they do not know how difficult it still is for me to find clothes that suit my body shape and my petite frame, and that hide the many scars all over my back that I am still very self-conscious about. I have always hated the word 'hump' because, at various points in my life, people have asked me, 'What is that big hump on your back?' Occasionally, I hear the word 'hump' in a completely different context – like when someone refers to Wednesday as 'hump day', meaning that once it is over, the week is rolling downhill towards the weekend – and I wince, because that word has nothing but negative connotations for me. The ironic thing is that, while for most of my life I refused to think of myself as having a disability because I did not want to feel weak, accepting that I do, and learning how to use the word 'disabled' about myself, actually makes me stronger. For a long time I did not see that the amazing life I have created for myself is precisely because I am strong enough to live with a disability and do everything I want to anyway. For years, as I said before, I had zero interest in settling into a long-term relationship with a man, partly because of my difficulties with my body image – and I still know that I will be perfectly happy if I never do – but having come so far towards accepting my complicated past, and my complicated present, for the first time in my life I am actually open to the possibility.

All my life, people have told me that I should write a book because so many different things have happened to me over the years, and because my background, and my physical reality, are so unusual. I never took those suggestions that seriously, partly because my life was always so full that there was never time and partly because I just did not think of myself as interesting enough. But during that strange period of lockdown, of reflecting on my past, and of my contact with the commission into mother and baby homes, I started to take the idea seriously for the first time.

The thought of making my story public was quite frightening, but I began to wonder if maybe it might be useful to other people. If the experiences that I have had might shed some light on what it is like to be Black or mixed-race in Ireland today, and what it is like living with a visible disability. Perhaps, I thought, opening up about my experiences would help others understand where people like me are coming from, and even make it easier for them to adapt their behaviours in ways that will help us all.

Maybe, I thought then, writing this book would be good for me too. Perhaps it would help me to understand myself better, to process the various traumas that I have always struggled to keep suppressed, and to move into a new and exciting phase of my life in which there are no more secrets.

I was extremely anxious when my piece on the Black and Irish feed was published, when I was interviewed on *The Ryan Tubridy Show*, and when the BBC featured my story alongside those of Conrad and Jude. As I write, I know that my stomach will be absolutely full of butterflies when this book comes out and is reviewed by the papers. I will be nervous and worried that I am making myself too vulnerable, that some of the people who read it will find it annoying or challenging in a way they do not like, and will make negative comments about it. But behind all that, I know that I can take it.

I always felt that I wanted to be very strong and very independent, because I did not want people to feel sorry for me. I think I thought that I was pretending to be strong, because I had no choice. I was not able to see the strength I really do have. But now, at last, I can.

Nobody has any control over how they are born, and the family they grow up in, and I am no exception. In fact, I have never felt exceptional at all. It was only when I really started to reflect on my life – the circumstances of my birth, the fact that I am Black and Irish, my scoliosis – that I realized I *am* exceptional. While I am not a public persona – not famous, not rich – my life has been truly extraordinary.

That realization has given me a great sense of obligation

to speak out about my experiences as a child of the Irish mother and baby homes, as a Black Irish woman, as an adoptee, and as a person who lives with disability.

My experiences give insight into not just what I have lived through, but into what it means to be Irish today and how we can collectively come to terms with and make sense of our shared history, while building a better future for us all.

13. A Call to Action

So, the big question is: what can ordinary people like you and me do to make our society, our country, a better place? I think accepting that we have a problem with racism, and beginning to tackle it, would be a good start, because if we cannot accept people from all sorts of backgrounds as equals, who deserve the same sort of respect and care as we do, we will never see progress.

For centuries, and right up into my own childhood, Ireland was a poor country from which people fled in search of exactly the same sort of opportunities that Ireland's new residents are seeking for themselves now. Poor Irish people flocked into the run-down areas of British cities like Liverpool, Birmingham and London, and American and Canadian cities like Boston, New York, Chicago and Montreal. They went to Australia and New Zealand, Argentina and Chile. They went all over the world, finding areas with low rent and cheap housing to open little businesses and start their new lives. Their hard work and dedication rejuvenated desolate inner cities and brought new life to down-at-heel neighbourhoods and towns. In other words, those Irish emigrants were *exactly the same* as the people coming to Ireland from faraway places now, to work as taxi drivers, cleaning ladies, waiters and so on.

When we Irish talk about our history, we discuss our diaspora with enormous pride: the Irish Americans, Irish Canadians and Irish Australians who went on to achieve great things, or the Irish Londoners – like the Pogues – who have brought our traditions, our culture and our love of music to the attention of an international audience and given us the reputation for warmth and musicality that has made the Irish loved around the world, and inspired the opening of a hundred thousand Irish pubs. In my own beloved Dublin, the Epic Museum on the docklands, which tells the story of Ireland's diaspora, is regularly feted as one of the country's best tourist destinations, and it is very moving for the descendants of that diaspora, now Americans or Canadians or Australians or whatever, to visit Epic when they are on their holidays and learn about all that their ancestors endured to give them a better life.

Of course, we are dead right to be proud of those people, because they worked so very hard for everything they got, and while Irish people abroad have never faced racism on the scale that Black people have, they did have to deal with discrimination and with the troubled legacy of the colonial period in Ireland. But we should also be proud of the other people. The ones who came here from somewhere else. The ones who do not look like 'us'. The ones who work so hard to achieve all that they do despite the tidal wave of racism that they are swimming against, every single day of their lives. We should be proud of them because, of all the destinations in the world, they have chosen our rainy little island to be their home and the place in which they will work as hard as they can to make their dreams come true. Their children will grow up learning Irish, knowing the rules of hurling, and representing Ireland in football and at the Olympics. They will support Ireland in the World Cup. If they move overseas when they grow up, they will pine for Tayto crisps and soda bread. Whether they speak Polish or Swahili, French or Urdu at home, they are Irish too – and a lot of them are Black and Irish, just like me.

'There's so *many* of them coming over now,' I heard people say in the 1990s as immigration into Ireland rose from its previous minuscule levels, and as I started to experience for the first time what it felt like to walk down Dublin's Grafton Street and not be the only Black person there, 'there'll be nothing Irish left.' People still say that today, and it is a mark of how self-righteous they are on this topic that they often do not feel even a little bit ashamed to say it right in front of someone who looks like me, and sometimes even expect me to agree with them.

I did not agree, back in the 1990s, that Ireland is threatened by people whose origins are elsewhere. Not at all. And I still do not. I have too much respect for Ireland and Irishness. I believe that Irish culture, in all its complexity, is strong and vibrant. I do not believe that our culture and traditions are threatened by the presence of people who started their lives somewhere else. In fact, I know that the opposite is true. Our culture and traditions are vibrant and strong and a bit of immigration is not going to change that. A hurling team that features players with surnames not seen as typically Irish is as good as any other. A trad session that can accommodate African drums and East European rhythms alongside our bodhráns and tin whistles is a wonder to listen to. We can have bacon and cabbage one day and Vietnamese hot and sour soup or Nigerian fufu the next. I believe that we are stronger together than apart, and that we all have a lot to learn from one another.

One of the things that I love about the Black and Irish feed on social media that I encountered on my journey of self-exploration is the fact that it is an opportunity for all of us to learn about what it is like navigating two or more cultures in a single lifetime, and a place where I can share my experiences and compare them to those of others. For most of my life, I had been quite wary about discussing my position as a Black Irish woman with my friends and colleagues. I did not want to bore anyone, and I also felt that anything that had happened to me was nothing special. In conversation with others, I have learned that everyone's experiences matter, and that it is only by collating and understanding the evidence of many that we can truly understand the big issues. When it comes to a serious matter like racism, one person's experience can be dismissed as an outlier, but when lots of people testify about the things that have happened to them, it becomes much more difficult to minimize or ignore.

On the surface, it looks as though Ireland is trying to deal with racism. Schools and parents are concerned about the role that racist bullying can play in seriously damaging young people's mental health, and they have very good reason to be. The Internet, which can be such an incredible resource and tool in so many ways, is often weaponized in the form of toxic 'debates' on social media, and the spreading of misinformation, lies and hate. When people experience the endless repetition of racist stereotypes online, they can start to lose their shock value, and even to be absorbed into their worldview. Government ministers say all the right things, and there are lots of official policies and anti-bullying initiatives in schools and elsewhere. Thankfully, while a few extremists have been doing their best to launch political parties and movements that are explicitly racist, they have been getting relatively little traction.

But plenty of issues still remain, and less obvious forms of racial discrimination are both more difficult to legislate against and harder to pinpoint. For example, people with African-sounding names are less likely to be called to interviews than those with identical qualifications and Irish-sounding names. Although they should not have to, a lot of Africans adopt more European-sounding names when they are sending out their CVs in search of work. A lot of Black parents feel their hearts break when their child, having experienced racism at school or in the playground, says that they wish they were white, or that they do not like the colour of their skin or the appearance of their hair. Imagine being a little child and feeling that you want to change your own body just to fit in with a norm that people seem to find more acceptable; it does not bear thinking about, and yet it happens all the time.

Rather than burying our heads in the sand when it comes to racism in our country, we need to accept that racism is everywhere. It is in families, it is in work, it is on the streets and it is in shops. But it does not have to stay like that, because we can work together to make things better.

Talking about race, racism and discrimination in general is often seen as being very complicated. A lot of important issues, requiring urgent discussion and remedies, do not get the attention they need because people worry so much about being seen to do the wrong thing that, instead, they do nothing at all. However, I believe there are lots of things that we can do that will make a big difference to us, and to our whole society, every day.

The first step towards making positive change is admitting that there is a problem. A lot of people in Ireland are in denial about the extent to which racism and other forms of discriminatory behaviour are a problem here. Are there places that are worse than Ireland? Definitely. But that is not the point. We cannot do much to address problems of discrimination elsewhere, but we *can* all work together to make Ireland a better place for everyone who lives here by ensuring that we approach life in a positive way. The thing is, we need to act quickly, and we need to develop a zero-tolerance approach to racism and other forms of discrimination, because discrimination in Ireland has acquired a new edge as far-right movements and even mainstream politicians around the world have become more overt in their racist views, and a lot of previously latent racism is increasingly coming to the surface.

Until recently, while racism has always been a problem in Ireland, efforts to establish and organize an explicitly racist political party have faltered and failed. Today, those efforts are gathering steam, and it is becoming more common to see groups of racist zealots protesting on the streets and on social media. Somehow, we have to find a way to make this stop. We need to understand that those who migrate or immigrate to Ireland are just like the Irish abroad: people in search of a better future for themselves and their families. Fortunately, there are *lots* of ways in which we can step in to ensure that racism does not gain ascendance in our country, as it has in others.

Clearly, it is essential for schools to have anti-racism policies, as of course they do – but much more important than that is discussing these issues in the home. There is little point in teaching children in school about treating everyone equally when at home they are being told that some people are better than others, just because of what they look like. Parents can make a point of discussing diverse cultures and traditions in a positive way.

We can all make a point of shopping in businesses that are proactive in supporting equality and of voting for politicians who go beyond lip service when it comes to matters of race and racism.

We can establish laws and social norms that respect our right to free speech while also protecting our right not to be the target of hate speech.

We can demand that our national television and radio broadcaster works harder to reflect our increasingly multicultural society, and we can insist that public bodies like the civil service and the gardaí engage with minority communities to ensure that they are represented at every level of our society, and that young people growing up learn to see all sorts of faces as the face of authority.

We can take a critical look at how we care for some of the most vulnerable people amongst us – the large numbers of asylum seekers in direct provision, many of whom are people of colour – and ask whether, on some level, our government feels that the conditions they live in are acceptable because most of them are not white.

By making racism and other forms of discrimination unacceptable, we can start to make dramatic change. Going beyond explicit racism, we can start to think about the many ways in which we can show respect and care for others. By making the effort to learn how to pronounce an unfamiliar name, we show someone that we respect them as an individual. We can challenge ourselves, or others, when racism or belittling comments are passed off as humour. We can think carefully about the language that we ourselves use to talk to and about others.

We can use social media to represent a positive view of the world, rather than as a way of airing our grievances and getting into spats with strangers. When we make mistakes, as we all do, we can apologize, learn and move on, rather than resort to defensiveness. We need to force ourselves to be strong enough to confront the bullies, because nobody can do that all on their own. We can ensure that everyone is visibly and tangibly represented at every level of our society.

In order to make dialogue easier, we have to create an atmosphere in which people can step up and do their best to make positive change without panicking that they will be slapped down by people who enjoy feeling better about themselves by making others feel small. It often seems that people agonize about and devote a huge amount of attention to issues that should not be important, while completely ignoring the things that matter most.

I see lots of people working themselves into frenzies over the idea that only Black people should be able to work in development agencies working with other Black people, and even casting aspersions on white people who do important development work in Black majority countries, and saying that they are just trying to make themselves look good. Yes, I know that the idea of the 'white saviour' who has to save Black people from their fates is a dangerous one that needs to be considered – but that does not mean that no white person should ever work in a development agency or a charity just because the people it supports are Black. I mean, seriously?

I have even heard people casting scorn on white parents who adopt Black and mixed-race children and suggesting that this should not even be legal and that they are being racist by assuming that they can provide such a child with a suitable home. Again, yes, I know that ideally children will grow up and be cared for in the culture into which they are born – but sometimes they cannot, and sometimes, like me, their origins are complex and they do not fit neatly into any single category. Should I have languished in an institution until an adoptive couple from Ireland and Zambia was ready to take me in? How dare people suggest that a family's love for one another is somehow less valid if they do not all have a similar appearance? I would like to hear someone trying to say that to my mam and dad. They would not last very long, I can tell you that.

We also have to learn how to be less judgemental when people who are doing their best inadvertently say or do something 'wrong'. It is crazy, but a lot of fantastic people of all colours are actually afraid to speak out about race and racism because they are not confident in their ability to do so with the vocabulary that is currently considered correct. They are afraid of saying anything about it at all on social media in case someone takes offence at well-meant words and starts a vicious pile-on. Honestly, I am often afraid of making a wrong step myself – and I am actually Black! I can totally understand the anxieties of those who worry that they might say the wrong thing, and clearly something is broken if people are too scared to even bring up important subjects.

I also feel that people often find it much easier to agonize over issues like 'cultural appropriation' – a concept that I have never seen adequately defined, and that I could easily be accused of myself, for making meditation such an important part of my life – and attack others for doing something that they feel is politically incorrect rather than dealing with the systemic racism that is the real problem. When I got my hair straightened for the first time, Dad teased me and called me Pocahontas. He was referring to the cartoon of the same name, and the lead character's flowing hair. If he said the same thing today, someone might jump down his neck and accuse him of making light of the situation of the Native Americans. Obviously, Dad meant nothing of the sort, and even if the movie's interpretation of the historical events it is supposed to show is not perfect, that is not his fault.

It is quick and easy to organize an indignant pile-on on the Internet because you have decided that someone's hairdo or dress is cultural appropriation, but actually examining your own personal prejudices and those of your society, not to mention addressing them, is very hard work. Yes, I am utterly opposed to the so-called 'cancel culture' and view it as an enormous barrier as we try to work towards the inclusion and understanding that most of us would like to see.

Because people of European descent have long dominated so much of the world and held so much of the power, it can be tempting to think that tackling white racism is the only thing that matters. Obviously, white racism is a huge problem, and of course it needs to be confronted and dealt with head-on. But I also believe that people from all sorts of backgrounds and of all races and origins need to engage in some self-exploration to understand how racism has touched their lives, to examine their own prejudices, and to advocate for themselves, their communities and for all of those who would benefit from support.

Tolerance is not enough – when we 'tolerate' people we are saying that we are putting up with them, that we may not like the situation, or them, or what they do and think and say, but we are willing to accept it for the sake of peace. Who really wants to be 'tolerated'? Minorities of all sorts need acceptance, not toleration.

In some ways, Ireland is in a very fortunate position when it comes to grappling with issues of racism. Because Ireland was a relatively poor country for so long, we had very little immigration when other Western countries were experiencing lots of it. This means that we can look to them, see what they did wrong and what they did right, and learn from it. We have the opportunity to build on the experiences of others and also from the mistakes that we have collectively made in the past and, hopefully, to do a better job of accommodating change and adapting to it in a positive way. This is important, and it is also urgent, because we are still making a lot of mistakes, perhaps most seriously in terms of how we provide shelter to asylum seekers. With our long and tarnished history of institutional 'care', abusive mother and baby homes, and cruel industrial schools, I cannot understand why we have adopted a model of provision for asylum seekers that seems to be based on an age-old system that has become another of Ireland's greatest sources of collective shame. We can also learn from the many mistakes that have been made in the past regarding the Irish Traveller community, which has long experienced a form of racism that has nothing to do with the colour of Travellers' skin.

Of course, racism and other forms of discrimination based on race and ethnicity are only one part of a bigger issue, which is dealing with difference in general, and learning how to see difference as just fine, and not as a challenge to the established norm. Also fundamental, therefore, to building a more equal society is accommodating people with physical difference in the form of disability. Again, our politicians say all the right things, and of course a lot of progress has been made in this area and people with disabilities are more included in schools, universities and workplaces than before, but there is still a great deal of work to do.

Much of this involves examining our own personal reactions and responses to disability, and to ensuring that people with disabilities feel and see themselves represented as valuable and valued members of society. Of course, it is wonderful that so many more buildings and modes of public transport are now wheelchair accessible, and it is great that our towns and cities are slowly becoming friendlier places for people who cannot see, and it is fantastic that supermarkets are beginning to have 'quiet evenings' for people with autism who find doing their shopping stressful otherwise. But just as I rarely encountered images of mixed-race girls like me when I was growing up, disabled people see very few positive images of people living with disability.

I remember how much it meant to me as a teenage girl when Benetton used gorgeous Black girls to advertise their clothing, and I can only imagine how much it would have meant if, once in a while, they had used a model with an obvious physical disability. I would love to see young people growing up with physical disabilities and differences today having role models to look up to. Of course, once every four years we all get to see the incredible athletes in the Paralympics, and that is brilliant, but it is not nearly enough. Like most people without disabilities, most people with disabilities are never going to be world-class athletes like the Paralympians. They still deserve to see people who look like them living full lives in public and to know that their disability, while part of who they are, is only a tiny piece of the whole picture.

More exposure to images and representations of people with disabilities and physical differences would have a big positive impact for people like me, and it would also do a world of good to everyone else. Anyone with an obvious physical difference can tell hundreds of stories about the comments and questions they have to deal with practically every single time they go out to get some shopping or post a letter. One of the issues that people with physical differences of this sort come up against all the time is that people like to comment on their appearance and ask about why they look the way they do. Sometimes they can be quite hostile, but most often they think that they are being jovial or friendly when they ask you if you were in an accident or whether you are walking funny because you got out of bed on the wrong side. This can be stressful, hurtful and just plain offensive to someone who is trying to get through their day.

We need to understand and appreciate that these sorts of comments, just like racist comments, underline and enforce a power imbalance, and that they often serve to keep people in their place. Just as it makes women feel uncomfortable and threatened when men comment on their bodies in public, or touch them without their permission, and just as it can be intimidating or frightening for people from a racial minority to have to deal with constant comments about their appearance, or have their hair touched or stroked without their permission, disabled people have the right to go through their lives without strangers commenting on how they look or move, no matter how well-intentioned those strangers think that they are being.

People who stand out because of their physical appearance for whatever reason need to assert their right to exist in public without having to go to lengths to make other people feel more comfortable around them. If people feel awkward around a Black person, that is their problem. The Black person has no responsibility to answer questions about where they are from and what they are doing here if they do not feel like it. If people feel awkward around a disabled person, that is their problem too. The disabled person does not have to make them feel better by entering into a conversation about why they have the issues that they do or by laughing at their awkward and insensitive remarks about the disabled person's physical appearance.

Speaking for myself, after a lifetime of dealing with strangers' questions interrupting my nights out with friends, my trips to the supermarket and my forays on public transport, I have had enough. I have started asserting my right not to deal with them at all. I have started to say, 'I don't feel like answering that' and 'That's a personal question that I don't want to discuss.' I have started to understand that if their feelings are hurt by my refusal to divulge my life story on demand, that is their issue, not mine.

At the end of the day, though, the most important thing is not to understand the complex ins and outs of racism and of disability and equality rights, but to approach life with empathy, because when we view others with empathy, we cannot help but see them as the complex beings that they are.

When we place empathy at the centre of our lives, we have no choice but to examine our own prejudices – and yes, we all have prejudices, even those of us who ourselves belong to discriminated-against minorities, and we all make mistakes. When that happens, we do not have to engage in a chest-beating exercise, but rather see it as an opportunity to learn. For example, I do not think that my family and I are awful people because we used to have a golliwog doll – but I do think that, now we know about the history of the toy, we should not get another one.

When we place empathy at the centre of our lives, we can correct people without the angry self-righteousness and the 'cancel culture' that dominate social media, and we can self-correct without becoming self-loathing and angry. We can accept that sometimes we will get things wrong too, and that it is OK if someone says, 'Actually, please don't call me that,' or, 'I'm not comfortable with how you're talking to me.' Everyone makes mistakes, and we can all learn new habits.

A lot of people study issues of race, racism, disability and human rights in universities, and lots of big, complex theories have been developed to explain why our societies have evolved to be the way they are. I know that this work is tremendously important and has its place in the conversation, but when all's said and done, if we want a better society for everyone, the answer is actually very simple.

The old teaching, which is at the heart of countless religions and philosophies, that we should do our very best to treat others as we ourselves would like to be treated, is as valid today as it ever was. And, in the end, it is all we really need.

Acknowledgements

Mam, Dad and Ciara, this memoir is not only because of your love, support and nurturing of me, but it's my thank you to you for helping me be the person I am today.

My family and friends throughout the years; if you know me, you know my love for you is eternal.

Dave De Valera, my old friend, thank you for believing in me, and for giving me the pep talk and confidence to send my book proposal out to publishers. Making that first step of telling you about my book idea, and sending you my proposal for your opinion, was extremely nerve-wracking, but you were the voice of encouragement and support from that moment on.

Deirdre Nuttall, you mentored me throughout my entire memoir-writing journey, and I will never forget your expertise, empathy and guidance. Thank you doesn't seem enough.

Charles McQuillan, award-winning photojournalist and stringer for Getty Images, I was so delighted that you agreed to shoot my book cover. It's been a huge honour to be photographed by you again since our BBC shoot, and to know you. Thanks also to Al Mennie for assisting on shoot day. Much fun was had, and friendships formed.

Deputy Director of Sandycove, Patricia Deevy, Managing Director, Michael McLoughlin, and the whole Penguin team: thank you for believing in me and my book and for offering me my first publishing deal, as well as for your encouragement and mentorship throughout the writing process. I am extremely proud to be an author with such a prestigious publisher.

Grá,
Marguerite xx